DISCOVERING WHO I AM
FROM A LIFE
LIVED & LEARNED

ANUP GAWDI

First published in 2020 by

Becomeshakespeare.com

One Point Six Technologies Pvt Ltd.
119-123, 1st Floor, Building J2, B - Wing, WadalaTruck Terminal,
Wadala East, Mumbai, Maharashtra, India, 400022.
T:+91 8080226699

ISBN - 978-81-947726-0-6

TABLE OF CONTENTS

Preamble	4
Introduction	6
Chapter 1 – Prioritize Things Based On One's Belief System	11
Chapter 2 – Who Am I?	15
Chapter 3 – My Elders	19
Chapter 4 – My Sister To My Cousins – True Mirrors	44
Chapter 5 – My Childhood Friends & My First School	57
Chapter 6 – My Core Group Of Friends	63
Chapter 7 – Meeta	91
Chapter 8 – My Juniors, Colleagues And Seniors	111
Chapter 9 – My Commandments	146
Chapter 10 – Family Management	151
Chapter 11 – Work Place Management	163
Chapter 12 – Managing & Nurturing Children	199
Chapter 13 – Adjusting to Our Society	209
Chapter 14 – Conclusion But At The Same Time A New Beginning	238

PREAMBLE

The world is affected by the Corona Virus (Covid19) and like the rest of the world; I am sitting at my home in a lockdown for the past 8 weeks doing nothing. In the nothingness of my house, the only thing left for me to do was reflecting on things gone by and the journey which I have had. The situation I find myself in makes me recollect a few lines I had heard somewhere,

Nature and Life Are AMAZING,

When you feel you have seen and learnt ALL

It shows you SOMETHING

That makes you REALIZE

What you have seen and learnt is just a FRACTION;

AND THERE ARE MILES TO GO…………..

The world is suffering, people are losing their livelihood, there is sadness everywhere, but there is something which I feel is happening for the first time in our human civilization history and that is, everyone is HOPEFULL that life will be better going forward.

Now coming back to my world, amongst all this nothingness, life seems to have given me something which I always wanted "TIME TO REFLECT".

For someone who decided to quit his job of 19 years, 12 months ago to return to India, to be with his family, attend to some family matters and see if he can make something out of himself again from scratch, this lockdown provided the perfect opportunity to reflect on things gone by, for me.

Meeta also kept insisting that since I have a way with words, I could try my hand at writing. Yes, I used to write but that was a long time ago and had not written anything for quite some time.

But a thought came to me, 'The life I have lived and the lessons I have learnt from the experiences I have had, could make for some interesting reading'. This thought resulted in this try which you are about to read.

My writing might be amateurish and the structure of the book bad, but at least I shall be able to say that I tried and if I can get a couple of laughs out of you from my stories or if I can get even a single person thinking for a minute, I think I would have achieved something.

INTRODUCTION

From a little boy in a quite Mumbai suburb to an NRI and back, from being a Date Entry Operator to a Regional Director and then back, from getting married at a young age of 22 to being married for close to 23 years, the one thing I can safely say is that, 'A decent life I have lived'. At close to 45 years of age, the one thing I can also say is that I have at least some life experience and stories which I can share with you.

For me life has been all about moving ahead, it is like time, it never stops. And Living Life is all about understanding how to keep moving.

As a person rebooting his life various thoughts kept running through my mind.

The thoughts which however kept coming up, over and over again were,

- "Why did I behave in this manner when I was faced with a particular situation?" and

- "Why did I choose the option I chose to come out of the situation?"

I am sure every one of us ponders on this at some point or the other and this lockdown, provided me ample time to do the same.

On further probing inside me, I realized one thing about myself and that was I never liked to complicate things.

Always trying to look at situations from a perspective of how I can cause least damage, first of all to myself, 'like it is always said self-preservation is best preservation and even the airlines stipulate this while making their safety announcement asking passengers to wear their mask first before helping others' and then the least damage to someone else.

When I realized this I became aware of something else. I understood because I wanted to keep life simple, I had subconsciously developed very simple formulas in my mind on which I have lived my life always and continue to do so even now, which is :

LIFE = Moving Ahead

Moving Ahead = Adapting

Adapting = My Action

(Learning = Positivity + Self + People)

My Actions = Who I Am

I Am = Sum (My Beliefs)

My Beliefs = Sum (My Experiences)

So LIFE IS = SUM (OF MY EXPERIENCES)

Learned people have always said Life is Simple, It is we people who have complicated it. Since we the people have complicated it, it is in our hands to start un-complicating it as well.

To make life simple, my formulas are good enough and I am sure quite a few of you who are reading this will be using these formulas in your life as well, some subconsciously and some with a clear understanding of them.

For those who are using these formulas subconsciously, hopefully my experiences which I shall be narrating you now, shall help what is subconscious become the conscious.

But since I am not a great writer, I am sure quite a few of the subconscious minds shall continue to remain as subconscious minds, but at least it would be a lesson learnt to these subconscious minds that one should never waste money on buying a book about someone else's life lived, especially if that someone is a nonentity.

However, I am also sure about one thing and that is, we all like to peek into someone else's life and you will definitely be inquisitive to get into my life as well.

So, let me take you into my world, my Simple Complicated World, where I shall introduce you to the people who made me 'Who I Am' and how my belief system helped me manage the challenges which life put forth and how through these experiences I became what I Am.

For me the belief system is the foundation on which the Building of Life is created. Like any building apart from the foundation there needs to be pillars which gives the Building of Life its shape. Pillars accordingly to me are the preferences or priorities that a person has in his life.

Life is all about making choices and it is good to know your priorities as it helps to prevent a very bad habit which is growing in our society now a days and that is Frustration.

Since every journey needs to start from somewhere, I think introducing you to my pillars would be a good place, as probably it shall help you to understand how the problem of Frustration can be managed since it is all around and I think it is a good place to start this journey from.

Chapter 1 - Prioritizes Things Based on One's Belief System

Since I said I shall try and help prevent you from becoming frustrated in your life; my simple solutions for this is always know what your priorities are and always remain true to them.

My definition of Priorities is nothing but the pillars around which one builds his/her life, simple right?

Saying one needs to prioritize, is easy but for getting your priorities right is a different story in itself. Similarly, it is easy to say you need to know your priorities but finding out what these priorities are is a different matter altogether.

My solution for prioritizing is also simple, whatever makes you most happy comes higher up in your list of priorities.

Hopefully by going through my example, a bell might ring in your head and will help the subconscious become the conscious.

The 3 Most Important Pillars of my life, in order of priority are,

1. My Family

2. My Friends

3. My Work

But these are my priority list and there are no hard and fast rules for prioritising or what your pillar should be. All one needs to do is to be true to themselves and the problems of your life can be avoided.

The problem comes when you start working against your priorities; conflicts arise in your mind which is followed by frustration. Identifying your priorities helps you to develop a mechanism whereby you can prevent this frustration from developing.

Prioritizing one's life based on his pillars helps solve one aspect of my life's simple formula. Every time I decided on what I needed to do, I looked up my priority list and took decisions which are closest to my hierarchy.

<u>My Actions = What are my Priorities = Who I Am</u>

If I take a decision which goes against my priorities it shall affect me in a way which shall make me unhappy and then lead to my frustration, so to keep frustration away and me smiling all I need to do is keep my actions as close as possible to my priorities.

Giving you an example of how this formula works is, if I am a family man and I need my entire family around me all the time to feel secure, placing me in an environment away from my family for too long shall make me go crazy.

Giving you another example on how situations also affect you is, 'If you are an extrovert person always surrounded by friends and suddenly if you are made to sit in a lockdown as the one being implemented globally when I was writing this book, you shall be very frustrated, but similarly if you are a family man wanting to spend time with your family you shall think this is the best thing which you could have asked for'. Same situation but because the priorities are different, effect is different.

<u>So Your Actions = Who You Really Are</u>

I have already told you what my top three commitments are in terms of my pillars (Family, Friends, Work), but I need to make you understand within these Pillars also there needs to be a priority setting.

This is because 'Time' is something which is limited and you are always expected to choose between who comes first and second all the time. Knowing your internal self is nothing but establishing this hierarchy.

In your Family also you cannot just generalize. In my instance my Family comprises of My Parents, My Elders, My Wife, My Kids, My Sister, My Cousins and Myself, so I need to set this hierarchy as well in my head.

Similarly when it comes to friends, I am sure you have a hundred friends but whom amongst these hundred you consider more valuable will need to be established and finally at work as well, whether my seniors are more important to me or my team mates I need to establish that also in my mind, to ensure that whenever I choose one above the other I am being true to my priority listing.

Till here everything was very simple and your choices shall effectively answer your priority list for you. But now comes the tricky part on how one can explain 'Who Am I?'

WHO AM I?

WHO AM I?

AM I A NAME!

AM I A SURNAME!

AM I A DESIGNATION!

WHO AM I?

AM I A HUSBAND!

AM I A SON!

AM I A FATHER!

WHO AM I?

I AM ALL OF THE ABOVE

AND I AM NONE OF THEM

SO,

WHO AM I?

WHO AM I?

Chapter 2 - WHO AM I?

Explaining this again can be done in two ways. First being 'What I Think I Am' and second being 'What Others Think I Am'.

If I am to say what I am, then I am,

- Dedicated to whatever I am committed to

- A person who believes that when you love something the best way to show your love is being protective about it.

- A person who needs a place where I can be what I am and don't need to present myself as someone else

- A person who is greatly influenced by Ramanand Sagar Ji, B R Chopra Ji, Manmohan Desai ji, Hrishikesh Mukherjee Ji & Manohar Shyam Joshi Ji

And my Belief System is,

- Keep Life Simple

- Always Be Respectful

- Never Give Up

- Stay Committed

- Never Try And Do Anything Wrong

- Trust Your Family, Friends And Team And Always Be There For Them

- Never Compromise When It comes To Your Family

- Always Plan For A Rainy Day

- Try To Be Happy

Very idealistic right? But since I am the writer I can put anything I want to and since that's the case why not put the best stuff available in the market.

The Second way of describing 'Who I Am' can be done by people who know me and are kind enough to buy this book, read it and provide me as well as others their opinions about whether my understanding of "What I Am" is true or not

But since the second way shall come only after I have got my family and friends to buy the book, I would at least be confirmed as the smartest of them all, for managing to do the impossible and that is getting them to buy a book.

But one thing I can do is tell you what one of my friends Sunny Boy told me when he did my handwriting and signature analysis.

- I am 'Too Family Oriented' and I place my family above myself

- I am a stickler for rules and breaking rules is something I cannot do

- I always live my life within set boundaries

I am sure Sunny Boy will not be making this up as he is a trained Graphologist and when he did my analysis he had passed out.

I think he does know something about this topic as he

experimented on himself as well and changed his signature when he completed his course.

The things I have mentioned above are actually some of the things I have derived from my life experiences and are forming a small part of my belief system in reality, so I have not just picked up the best stuff available, I have actually experienced them and how I got them is all what my life till now is all about.

I strongly believe that what you turn out to be has a direct connection with your set of influencers and the experiences you have with them. Every child when he is born is like a piece of wet clay; it has all the genes to be moulded into something magnificent but is waiting for the mould to be cast. The mould is continuously getting cast by the people whom he or she comes in contact with, believes in and experiences encountered with them and it is this mould which becomes his/her core belief system.

Since a belief system is too intricate a part of oneself as everyone's experiences are different, I cannot touch base on your belief system as that is for each individual to identify their own, but I shall be showing you how I derived my belief system.

For my belief system to develop in the manner it has, I will take you on a long journey starting from when I was 3 years old to around 35 years of age. It is in this journey that my "Commandments" of life were finalized which helped me to cope with the challenges that life had thrown at me.

It's not that my learning process has been completed or my belief system established in stone, it is just that my core mould was cast by the time I turned 35.

Chapter 3 - My Elders

My story begins when I was 3 years old as before that I was just too small to remember anything.

It seemed I was born in an affluent house; my father was the eldest of 6 siblings (4 Brothers and 2 Sisters). I say it seemed, because when you are a child, you do not look at life from a monetary perspective. You look at it from a perspective of whether your needs are being fulfilled and if they are, you belong to a well to do family. From a child's perspective if you closely observe, every child feels it belongs to a well to do family as every parent fulfils their needs.

My family is a strange one. Age and Family Hierarchy just do not match.

- My grandmother was the eldest of her 6 siblings (2 Sisters and 4 Brothers) and her youngest brother was younger to her eldest son.

- My father was the eldest of 6 siblings (4 Brothers and 2 Sisters) and his youngest sister was 7 years elder to me.

- My mother was the eldest of 4 (2 Sisters and 2 Brothers) and her youngest brother was also just 7 years elder to me

Someone is someone's Uncle, but younger than him, someone is someone's brother/sister but treated as their son/daughter. All this is probably due to the fact that entertainment was missing in the world at that time and marriage at an early age was the practice.

To live in a joint family comprising of 13 members and a plethora of relatives marching in and out, one needed a huge house and that is what we had. A massive 8 bedroom bungalow in a quite suburb of Mumbai called Chembur.

From a child's eyes, the place looked massive. It felt as if there cannot be anything bigger.

The bungalow was located in a society comprising of 15 Bungalows and was at one end of a famous Golf Club. From our terrace we could see people putting and teeing off. There was a relaxation shed for tired golf players to have a beer or cold drink, it was from here where me and my friends climbed inside to collect the bottle caps. In the early and mid-1980's there were rewards which one could claim based on what was under the caps and I have exchanged these caps for comic books and even cold drinks during my childhood.

The festival celebrations and get-togethers at the society were great fun. Holi, Eid, Diwali, Christmas and New Year celebrations, we celebrated everything and that too together.

My grandmother although less than 5 feet tall was a dynamite. She was a very strong lady, capable of keeping things in check but she equally loved everyone. After India's independence when the family moved to Amritsar and then to Mumbai, she had the responsibility of running the entire household with her 6 Children, her mother in law and her mother in laws brother who was a bachelor all his life.

My grandmother ran the house with an iron hand. There is a story that I have heard that when my grandfather was falling short of money to buy the 8 bedroom bungalow, my grandmother took out a sizeable bunch of notes and gave it to my grandfather. When asked how she had so much money, she said she had been saving this amount since her Amritsar days from the money given by my grandfather to run the house.

Till her death, a couple of years back, she continued with this habit of saving up and believe me, when she left us a few years back, she still had a sizeable savings of a few lakhs left behind for us.

My grandmother was the driving force in the house and everyone had to listen to her. She believed in living life to the fullest. She missed my grandfather a lot after his death and kept a nice locket with my grandfather's photo in it right till the end, but she also continued to live life to the fullest. She loved clothes and every year without fail she used to try to change her wardrobe.

Since I never met my Grandfather, I have only heard stories about him. It is said he was one of the first to move to India after partition and set up a place of business in India. It is said he was like an aristocrat, always dressed properly with hair in place, a cigarette in hand and in the evenings he enjoyed his scotch. Due to my grandfather, our house in Mumbai was the first destination which welcomed anyone coming from abroad. It was because of my grandfather we had the best of things in the house as he believed in living life king size.

The story of my father's wedding is something which is unbelievable. If it was not for the video and photos, it would be difficult to even visualize it.

People in the late 1980, early 1990 started documenting their weddings in video, but my grandfather used a film crew in 1974 to make a movie on my father's wedding. He hired professional cameramen and photographers to document the entire journey from Mumbai to Udaipur (Rajasthan).

My grandfather took a group of around 150 people on this journey. The journey started at Mumbai Central station where 2 entire boogies / compartments were booked for the wedding party. In those days there were no pantries in the train, so our group were carrying cooks and entire food with them along with whole cans, filled with scotch along with water. It was a big party on wheels. The train took the group to Ahmedabad as there were no direct trains to Udaipur and from Ahmedabad the group took buses to Udaipur.

The wedding in Udaipur was the biggest party which Udaipur had never seen before. The groom side was put up at the only stadium in Udaipur as there were no hotel rooms available to cater to such a large group.

The match of my father and mother was fixed by my grandfather when he had seen my mother and the wedding took place at the town hall of Udaipur.

My grandfather expired within 5 months of my father's wedding following a massive heart attack. He was only 42 years old. My grandmother was around 39 with my father the eldest son who was 22, just married and with me on the way.

Since I was born after 6 months of my grandfather expiring, my grandmother took me under her wings and told everyone that I was her 7th child and took up the responsibility along with my mother of taking care of me.

She became my Badi Mummy and also Badi Mummy or Mummy Ma to all her grandchildren and great grandchildren. From daily baths and massages, to making me sleep with her, she was always around me.

My father's sisters who were only 7 and 9 years elder to me, used to sleep with me and my grandmother in her room. The room had a bed, which was the size of 2 king beds with a large window behind it.

Whenever, I was angry at not being told a story or when my father's sisters troubled me, I would go and sit behind the curtain and not come out of it till my wishes were complied with and believe me; 100% of the time they were complied with.

The relationship which I had with my father's sisters was more like the one which is shared between brothers and sisters. I called them Didi which means sister in Hindi. One was Raj Didi and the other was Sona Didi. Sona Didi the younger one started tying me Rakhie as well.

I was their youngest brother and they pampered me as well. In those days till early 1980's there was no TV and the only source of knowledge and entertainment were books and comics. So my earliest memories of my Didi's were reading their comics and going along with them to the book rental shops which were next to Chembur railway station or travelling with them along with my mother to fashion street in town or Linking Road in Bandra for doing their clothes and accessory shopping. The memories of sitting in a double decker bus all the way from Chembur to Fort are still very fresh in my mind.

My both Didi's have specific straits and are totally different personalities. Both are very talkative but Raj Didi has a very terrific sense of humour and her one liner were too much for a lot of people while Sona Didi was the innocent one always saying too much. Both of them got married early, Raj Didi when I was around 9 years and Sona Didi when I was around 11.

My mother was someone I love unconditionally as any son would. I will not say much about my mother except for the fact that whatever I became had a lot to do with what I learnt from my mother and how she brought me up and the lessons she taught me. She married very young, as soon as she completed her BA in Psychology but was quite mature in her handling of things even at such a young age.

As soon as she got married, she became the eldest Bhabhi to all the siblings of my father. She was and still is an outspoken person who still enjoys having a good laugh with her friends.

Like my father she was the eldest child of her parents and she had 3 other siblings with the youngest being just 7 years elder to me. My mother enjoyed and still enjoys her kitty parties and still has a big gang of girlfriends who are wives of my father's friends and relatives.

My Mummy tried her hand at learning to drive a car, did a course as a beautician but at the end of day she remained a house wife taking care of her family. If she had a career she would not have minded it but she wouldn't care less if she did not get it either. She was and is happy where she is.

My mother and father have a strange relationship; probably being married for 46 years does have its drawbacks. They fight like cats and dogs and are called the Hot and Cold Couple in our family but at the same time can't do without each other.

My father is someone I could not open up to in my initial years and even now it is difficult for me to do the same but I manage quite well now. The stories I hear of my father during his younger days seems that he liked to live a happy life, full of fun and enjoyment. The perfume collections of my father are something to be still envied off.

My father's style was greatly influenced by my grandfather and my grandmother's brother Prakash Mama or Bade Mama with whom he used to go and stay during his trips abroad. Since my father used to help my grandfather in his business during his college days, he used to travel abroad regularly for sourcing dry fruits and it is during these trips that he developed his style as well.

He also got into the habit of smoking and drinking during these trips as it was a fashion in those days.

My father believed in living life king size, probably influenced by his father and he was a good singer as well with a lovely voice. Unfortunately, I did not get these genes from my father, as I am an awful singer, but I did get some portion of it and that is listening to songs, especially soft Hindi numbers.

My initial memories of my father was he sitting at home with a glass of fine whiskey in one hand and a cigarette in another having Cheddar Cheese that he offered us kids.

My father's return from his foreign trips with bags full of gifts for his brothers, sisters and us was something we looked forward to all the time. He being the eldest was called Daddy by everyone, even his siblings. He was very social and enjoyed partying a lot with his friends.

His group of friends and relatives enjoyed their drinks thoroughly and celebration of Holi at our bungalow is something which I shall never forgot. As a family or with our group of relatives, there were numerous trips which I also cannot forgot, like the Shirdi Trip in a bus and a Matador, the Vaishno Devi and Mussoorie trip where entire hotels were fully booked for us as we were too many or the Khandala trips to Bushi Dam, which were truly enjoyable.

Daddy's routine when he was home was simple, every morning he would get up around 8 am, read the newspaper and have his bed tea with biscuits. Get dressed and have a heavy breakfast by 10:30 am. Leave for Chembur Station along with his younger brother to take a local train to Masjid Bunder for his office and return home by 8:00 pm. Once back he would freshen up and have dinner by 9:30 pm after that he would get his whiskey bottle out.

On Sundays the routine till Breakfast was the same with change happening post lunch when the beer bottles came out, prior to the whiskey in the evening. My interaction with my father initially was limited to getting my report card signed.

He was modern in his thinking but at the same time very conservative. Being educated he knew that the world was changing and the old patriarchal system was altering but the fight still was not won. It is this conflict which probably troubles him even today as he struggles to adjust himself to the ever changing world around him.

Being a person who was always listened to by everyone and his instructions followed without any questions asked, adjusting to a life where his siblings and kids have grown up and become independent in their thinking and lives, has been tough for him emotionally.

This proves my theory that one needs to be True To Oneself. For all of my father's socializing and partying's, the one thing which he probably gave most priority to was his family and when that family disintegrated, it affected him the most.

My father has gone through a lot in his life and the good thing is he still can manage a smile on his face and that is the best part.

One more thing I can say about my father is that, he is a very strong person. Just a few years back, when he realized his regular smoking was having an impact on his health, he managed to convince himself that he needed to give up smoking and he did it. From smoking almost 50-60 cigarettes every day to not a single one, hats off to him. Similarly, when his habit of drinking 6-7 pegs of whiskey everyday took a toll on his liver, he just gave it up. Giving up liquor did disturb him and continues to disturb him but he has been sober for more than 12 months while I am writing this book.

Now he even jokes, that giving up his smoking and drinking habits prior to the Corona Virus lockdown is the best thing he did as otherwise he would have been in deep trouble, like they say Whatever Happens, Happens for the Best.

My father's younger brothers are very different not only to my father but also from each other.

My father's younger brother Jagdish who is 2 years younger to him, whom I call Papa, was the quite one. He had a limited group of friends and even today the only people he calls his friends are those who have been his friends since his school / college days. When I was around one year old my Papa had just got married and I had a new Mummy on the block and I started calling her Pushpa Mummy.

The first set of memoires with Papa and Pushpa Mummy were sitting in their room every evening after dinner eating fruits, as my Papa loves fruits. Every night even today Pushpa Mummy sits with a tray of fruits which she cleans and peals and gives to Papa, her kids and grandchildren to enjoy.

With Papa my initial memories also pertain to playing various indoor games (carom, chess) and outdoor games (badminton, cricket, Frisbee) along with my other uncles, even my father used to join in these rounds of games. Our free times post dinner and fruits and on Sundays were these games and it was great fun always, my love for sports come from here actually.

With Pushpa Mummy, my memories are going to her parent's house in Collectors colony in Chembur camp area. The house was a small bungalow next to the RCF chemical factory and the fire burning on the top of the chimney in RCF was always a point of attraction to us but the best part of spending time at Pushpa Mummy's house was the amount of Pepsi Cola we had there and the stock which Pushpa Mummy used to get from her brothers factory.

Our refrigerator was always stocked with this Pepsi Cola and was the prime reason for my sour throat which bothered me all through my younger days.

My father's second brother Govind, whom I call Govind Chachu, was the scholar amongst all of them. He was the one pushing all those younger to him to study and become someone. He was 17 when I was born and by the time I turned 5 he had moved to IIT Kharagpur to study Engineering.

The first memories of Govind Chachu were all about his professional camera and his dark room as his passion and hobby was photography and still continues to be. We all children along with Sona Didi and Raj Didi were his models and our job was to pose for him.

Like I have said my grandfather was an aristocrat; he gave his children the best of things. Even after his death, my father continued to live life king size and ensured the children had the best of things whether it was the BOSE music system with big speakers or providing Govind Chachu with his camera and a dark room, you name any modern electronic which came in the market and it would find its way into our house immediately, whether it was a Colour TV, VCR or anything.

The song collections which Papa and Daddy had manged to collect, was extremely good, probably my habit of listening to old Hindi songs comes from here.

I clearly remember when in one of his vacations Govind Chachu decided to train me on how to use a professional camera with professional lenses. Those weeks were a torture for me. I being a child who always enjoyed the outdoors playing cricket or football or just being outside, was made to sit in a room with a camera which was difficult to hold with my tiny hands was a torture.

In those days there were rolls which were used not like today when you get trained on digital cameras which have auto focus, I was getting trained on a camera with lenses which needed manual tuning.

Since Govind Chachu did not want to waste rolls on me, he asked me to see outside, fine tune the lenses to ensure the vision is clear and handover the camera to him to check the view. I must say one thing about Govind Chachu; he did not give up on me.

He kept pushing me to somehow get that one perfect view and I must say, although I was not that great, I could fine tune a manual lens by the time Govind Chachu went back to his college.

Another hobby of Govind Chachu was collecting postal stamps and coins of various countries. The collection which he had with 3D stamps, stamps of different sizes, colours, shapes, was all very fascinating. In my childhood days seeing glimpses of other countries made all of us kids fall in love with the idea of travelling. Govind Chachu subsequently moved from India to US as it was his dream to make something of himself on his own esteem.

He was the first in our family to move to US to pursue post graduations and finally became an American citizen.

Govind Chachu married Jyoti Chachi whom he met in America at one of the Indian Family get-together organized by the Indian community there. Jyoti Chachi in a way is related to Pushpa Mummy as well. Jyoti Chachi's father was a doctor who had moved to US when she was a child in 1970's. Jyoti Chachi understands Hindi very well but owing to her upbringing in US, does not speak much in Hindi.

You should have seen the conversation which my Grandmother used to have with her when they used to meet, they were hilarious.

One thing about Jyoti Chachi is that she meets everyone with a very warm smile and a big hug and is genuinely a nice warm person. Getting along with a perfectionist like Govind Chachu is not easy but I am sure that Jyoti Chachi has found a way to handle him.

My other uncle, Ashok whom I call Ashok Chachu, was the cool one. He was youngest amongst the brothers and closer to his sisters and me. There are stories which are often mentioned in our family get-togethers about how Govind Chachu used to push Ashok Chachu, Raj Didi and Sona Didi to study and how all of them used to gang up on Govind Chachu to get away from him.

Govind Chachu being Govind Chachu probably got to Ashok Chachu finally and Ashok Chachu not only managed to get himself into a Medical College in Wardha but also topped his Post Graduations in Paediatric with a Gold Medal.

Why I call Ashok Chachu the cool one was because he had a cool set of friends growing up. In our society which comprised of 15 bungalows, most of the youngsters around were his age and they used to do some crazy stuff.

I remember the fun and fair which they had organized in Chembur. It was a one of a kind affair. To promote it and get people to come to the society, the group comprising of Ashok Chachu and his friends took out our Fiat car in the middle of the night and went about painting the address of our society and the date of the fun fair on each road and lane in Chembur. Since I could not be shrugged off as I was the stickler type, he had to take me along with him. It was absolute fun.

He was the first to have a full-fledged love marriage in the family. After his marriage not a single marriage in our family has been arranged including Govind Chachu's. He paved the way for my Love Marriage as well.

Ashok Chachu is now a very successful Neonatologist with a renowned Hospital in Navi Mumbai and my Vandana Chachi is a renowned Gynaecologist in Navi Mumbai.

Vandana Chachi was initially very quiet when she entered our family, probably shocked with the big bunch of people she had to interact with.

One thing I have to say about Vandana Chachi, she was and still is very warm to us kids. It is she who now insists that we all should meet regularly and if we do not catch up for a couple of weeks, she ensures that a get-together somehow gets organized were we all can meet and catch up.

One thing which was common amongst my father and all his brothers was that they always tried to do the right thing. They tried to be sticklers to the rules laid down, probably because it was the license Raj time in India when they were growing up.

Raj Didi and Sona Didi's husbands whom I call Jijajee were also in a way my set of influencers.

Raj Didi and Madan Jijajee moved abroad when I was around 12 but one thing which I remember very clearly was how fun loving Madan Jijajee was and is still is. He reminded me a lot of my Daddy with his style as he too believed in living life in style. The Limousine which he got for us for site seeing when we were visiting them proved that beyond doubt.

Sona Didi and Satish Jijajee, moved from Delhi to Goa and then went abroad to settle down. But with Satish Jijajee I was his smallest Sala. Satish Jijajee and for that matter his entire family are great singers and very good looking as well. I tried to copy Satish Jijajee's style a lot when I was small and like me, he too loved the movies.

Whenever Satish Jijajee would visit Mumbai or me Goa, we never failed to catch up a film in a theatre. At times it was just the two of us who used to go out as others would not be interested.

Another group of elders who influenced me initially were from my Mother's side.

My Mother being from Udaipur was entitled to a yearly break and allowed to spend close to 20-25 days every year during our summer vacation in Udaipur. My mother's father who we called Nanaji ran a typewriter institute in Udaipur and was a well-known figure in Udaipur. You would rarely find a person who did not know Diwan ji as he was popularly called.

My Nanaji owned a small Kothi (Bungalow) which he built from his own hard earned money, in a quite locality of Shastri Nagar. He had a very particular lifestyle. He used to get up early, get water arranged for the household, get dressed, eat breakfast, leave for his institute on his Rajdoot bike with his typical Dev Anand hat on his half bald head, come back home by 6:30 pm in the evening, get changed, have a single peg of whiskey with some savoury item, eat dinner, go for a walk, eat a pan, come back home and sleep. It was like clockwork.

He had his group of friends who everyday sat around his institute chatting and laughing. He lived a tough life, but one thing about him was, he was happy and always carried a smile on his face.

He had a strange sense of humour which was very dry. You would not realize he has cracked a joke on you as in the way he said it would feel like he has praised you.

While I was writing this book he expired on 14th April 2020 amidst the Corona India lockdown & something happened which cannot be explained. He always said the best way to cremate was the Arya Samaj way as he was not at all a religious person while all his family members, especially my Nani and my Mummy were very religious, my Mummy even today is totally religious. If it was not for the lockdown, my family would have cremated him the normal way, but due to it we had no option but to cremate him in the simple Arya Samaj way.

It's like he was waiting for the lockdown to happen and then breathe his last so that he goes the way he always wanted. It is well said in a Hindi film, "If you Desire Something with All Your Heart, The Entire Universe Works to Make It Happen". Not that he instigated the world to get the Corona Virus, but he survived till the time the corona virus came and that is destiny.

My mother's mother, my Nani was a beautiful and a very religious lady, a total opposite of my Nana ji. Even when she was old she had a beautiful smile. She was a typical housewife running the household.

Another trait of my Nani was that she avoided speaking to any of her Son-in-Laws. When they were around she was always quiet and covered her head with her Dupatta; strange but she was what she was.

My memories of my Nani were, she focusing on conserving water and ensuring we are kept nicely fat and healthy. Her pickles were just great, especially the one which she made with Onions.

Udaipur was a dry city and when we used to be there during our vacations which were during peak summers, providing water for everyone was tough. I remember going with her with utensils to the bore pump behind our Kothi and pumping it to draw water, filling the utensils and getting water to the house.

From seeing water flowing freely in our bungalow in Mumbai and seeing the trouble of sourcing water in Udaipur, convinced me that we need to conserve water and I took it upon myself that I would not waste it. So as an innocent child I decide not to have a bath every day and was prepared to get spanked by my mother for it, but I failed each time and every day.

My Nani also had a habit of tying money at the end of her Dupatta in a knot and whenever we kids needed money to buy snacks from the local vendors who used to carry stuff on their head or mobile carts and come into our narrow lane, all she used to do was untangle the knot, take out a couple of coins and tell us "Sab Mut Karsh Kar Dena" (Do not spend all of it).

It is only in her last years that I saw my Nani becoming weak with her emotions as probably she was not used to seeing her body fail her till such time.

My mother's younger sister got married to Vijay Jijajee when I was around 4 years old. We used to meet Lata Masi when she used to visit Udaipur with her kids when we also used to be there. Both sisters used to decide the travel dates based on their kids vacations in Mumbai and Delhi as she lived in Delhi while we lived in Mumbai. My memories with her are limited, but the one thing I do remember her with is her smile, she and my mother probably got their smile and beauty from their mother.

My memories in Udaipur were more with my mother's brothers.

Ravi Mama was a scholar as my Govind Chachu. He studied hard and completed his Chartered Accountancy and Company Secretary Courses and established himself as a good professional in his field, initially in Udaipur and then in Mumbai. He took from his father and had a very sarcastic sense of humour. He used to call us kids Khotas (Fools). I was greatly influenced by him and it was he who pushed me to take up commerce.

He married my Daddy's cousin sister and his match was arranged by my Mother and my Father. Kanchan Mami his wife was the same age as Sona Didi, therefore not only was she Kanchan Didi but also my Kanchan Mami. He taught me how to drive, gave me my first internship, taught me the basics of accounts and basically influenced me tremendously.

But Ravi Mama had a bad habit of disregarding things. When he got sick he took medicines only till he felt better, never completing his course. If a doctor told him to control his diet he just disregarded it.

His confidence in himself was tremendous. He always felt he can do no wrong and knew everything. Unfortunately he expired 3 years back due to health complication at a considerably young age. His death is something I cannot forgot as I felt he had more to give and left us too soon.

My mother's youngest was Narendra, whom everyone called Sonu. So he was Sonu Mama for me. He was more of a friend as he was just 7 years elder to me. I was his excuse to go out of the house in the evenings for a smoke. He also taught me to ride a two wheeler. He was always very ambitious and wanted to get out of Udaipur and he surely achieved it. Sonu Mama married Bobby Mami a match probably arranged by my Mom and Kanchan Mami. His energy levels are always on a boosted dose of adrenalin and whenever we meet, we meet as friends do and connect from where we had left off.

After reading all about my family members, you would be thinking why?

Like I have said at the beginning, my belief system comes from people I have interacted with and since my first set of interactors were my elders, I have tried to tell you in brief who they are and their peculiar traits .

Another important part of my early life was the Television and it's advent in the 1980's in our house which was an event that I can never forget.

The fascination of watching people coming live on a small little devise in your home was just magical. My addiction with TV from 1980's continues till date. It is my therapy.

The movies like Sholay, Naram Garam, Behraham and Messenger, DD serials like Ramayana, Hum Log, Buniyaad, Nukkad, Circus, Fauji, Yeh Joh Hai Zindagi, Star Trek, Hardy Boys, Nancy Drew, were my guides, my little windows to the world. I can get lost in these worlds any time.

When I was 14, mine and all others lives moved, first from Chembur's huge 8 bedroom bungalow to a much smaller 4

BHK Flat in Vashi Sector 3. From a 4 BHK in Sector 3 to a 2 BHK Rental Place in Sector 14 Vashi, to a 3 BHK flat on 3rd Floor of our Hospital and finally to 4 BHK in Sector 11, Koper Khairne.

My father and his siblings also moved on in their lives. With more and more people getting added into the family, keeping in check everyone's ambitions tied down was just not possible. No one was to be blamed for what happened to all of us. It was just that the world was changing and the nuclear bulb was being light inside our family as well.

There are some words of a famous poem which comes to my mind when I recollect my family time with my elders,

'Kabhi Kisi Ko Mukammal Jahan Nahin Milta

Kahin Zamin Toh Kahin Aasman Nahin Milta

Jise Bhi Dekhiye Voh Apne Aap Mein Gum Hain

Zubah Mili Hain Magar, Humzubah Nahin Milta

Bujha Saka Hain Bhala Kaun Waqt Ke Shole

Ye Aisi Aag Hain Jisme Dhuan Nahin Milta

Tera Jahan Mein Aisa Nahin Ki Pyar Na Ho

Jaha Umeed Ho Iski Wahan Nahin Milta'

In English it can be translated as below,

'No one gets the entire universe

Somewhere the Earth and Somewhere the sky is missing

Whoever you see is lost in their own sorrow

They have thoughts to share but no companion to listen

Who is able to douse the embers of time?

This is a fire that has no smoke

It is not like there is no love in your life (Universe)

Where you hope for it you won't find it there'

Luckily for us we could salvage something and that was thanks to Ramanand Sagar ji and BR Chopra ji who again came to our help. Their Ramayana and Mahabharata lessons at least kept the flame of unity burning, although all of us started living separately, the connections at time stretched however were not broken.

My father being the aggressive type after moving to Vashi moved to the construction business and Jagdish Papa took over the dry fruit business. My father became a builder and did a few good projects and also bought a hospital plot where he wanted to construct a hospital in the name of his father.

Since I was very young around 16, I can only speculate that there were some financial issues within the family owing to which the flat we were staying in had to be sold off and my Daddy moved to a rented accommodation.

For the next 18 months my father moved to a rented 2 BHK accommodation while Ashok Chachu too moved to a 2 BHK rented accommodation as they went their separate ways after the flat in Vashi was sold.

I could remember my Daddy moving from Scotch to Blended Whiskey from Foreign Cigarettes to Local Brand ones probably due to his financial issues.

I also remember Ashok Chachu starting a small hospital along with Vandana Chachi in Turbhe where I used to go for getting my fingers and my head fixed up which would keep getting damaged from catching the football and being kicked around.

Daddy's efforts were successful and after a tough struggle he completed the construction in 18 months and, we started using the top floor of the hospital as our residence.

Soon Ashok Chachu and Vandana Chachi also joined my Father and together they ran the hospital successfully for the next 17 years with me supporting the administration part slightly while also studying.

Even after the hospital commenced operations, there was something which was missing inside my father. He still enjoyed his drinks, but we could realise that he was inhibiting himself, not going out much. He used to and still comes alive when he is around his siblings and friends and whenever he is organizing things in a party or get-together. But again goes back to his shell when they leave.

Probably the financial crisis made my father a little bitter and till date something inside him still hurts when he recollects those days.

As for me, moving had a different set of challenges. First and foremost I had to adjust from an only boy's school to a co-ed boys and girl's school. Secondly I had to learn to make friends. I had very few friends while growing up in Chembur so making new ones was and is still a challenge.

My elders and the challenges faced by them which were not my challenges directly did affect me as I was a witness to them and they did shape me. My thoughts and beliefs are to a large extent by products of my time spent with them.

My Belief System picked up the following things from my experiences with my Elders,

- From my grandmother, father and Govind Chachu who probably picked up the same trait from their mother, I picked up the idea of never giving up from them.

- From my grandmother, always save something for a rainy day

- From Papa patience and the love for fruits and

- From Papa and all my Chachu's the love for sports

- From Ashok Chachu, Raj Didi, Sona Didi & Sonu Mama, the idea of fun and what parties with family mean

- From my nana ji and nani, how we can do with less as well and keep smiling

- From Ravi Mama how one should never be over confident and don't take life lightly.

- From my mummy, I understood the meaning of unconditional love.

- From my daddy, what it means to live life king size and how to always keep getting back up on your feet after life keeps pushing you down

- Finally from all of my elders I understood the True meaning of Family which is, it is complicated.

- Also finally I understood that TV does have a big influence on an impressionable mind, as I got Ramanand Sagar Ji and B R Chopra Ji imprinted in my mind 100%.

Chapter 4 - My Sister To My Cousins – True Mirrors

❖

Now let me come to my cousins and sister. Since my father had 6 siblings and my mother had 4 siblings, I am proud to say we are a bunch of 20 first cousins.

- My father has me and my sister Shweta who is 4 years younger than me.

- Papa and Pushpa Mummy have Meghana who is 3 years younger than me and Yash who is 7 years younger than me.

- Raj Didi and Madan Jijajee who were next to get married have 3 daughters, Neha who is 9 years younger to me, Niti who is 12 years younger to me and Bianca who is 22 years younger than me.

- Sona Didi and Satish Jijajee have two sons, Shashank who is 13 years younger to me and Shivek who is 15 years younger than me.

- Ashok Chachu and Vandana Chachi have Karan who is 14 years younger than me and Tanya who is 19 years younger than me.

- And finally Govind Chachu and Jyoti Chachi who were the last to get married have two sons, Rohin who is 20 years younger than me and Rahul who is 22 years younger than me.

- On my mother's side, my mother's younger sister Lata Masi has 3 kids, Mini who is 7 years younger to me, Gini who is 12 years younger to me and Dhruv who is 17 years younger to me.

- My mother's brother Ravi Mama and Kanchan Mami had 2, Vipra who is 15 years younger to me and Ashish who is 17 years younger to me

- And finally my mother youngest brother Sonu Mama and Bobby Mami have 2 kids, Mudit who is 20 years younger than me and Khushi who is 24 years younger than me.

Except for Meghana, Shweta, Mini, Gini, Dhruv, Khushi and Bianca I have received blessings from each of them in the form of their showers and I have put them all to sleep in my lap at least once. Since I have had the most experience with children of all age groups I am called the handler of kids in the family. Even today give me a new born kid and I can take care of them as long as they are not hungry for which I cannot do anything. I am extremely happy when I have a child in my arm.

Luckily for me, my cousins keep giving me this opportunity. As recently as just a couple of months back, thanks to Yash I have a new kid to take care of.

We all cousins are progressing in adding more numbers to our clan and our count of kids as on today stands at a healthy 15 with still around half of them to still register their numbers.

One of my friends seeing my DP on Facebook which was a photo of our entire clan in one of the latest weddings in my family commented this is not a family but a full village and believe me when we meet it is nothing less than a massive party.

Meghana, Shweta and I were a trio initially. I loved them a lot but also troubled them a lot. Meghana and Shweta have two different natures.

Meghana was the proper girlish one always well dressed with a nice haircut and all pretty as a doll. Shweta was the tomboyish one, with curly hair, chubby cheeks and anger at the tip of her nose.

Meghana used to start crying immediately on being troubled, but on the other hand Shweta would hit me first, then realize that she is a girl and start crying. Given a chance even today Shweta would still hit me for the trouble I caused her, but Meghana would probably sit with me and explain things.

With Meghana, my first memory is of having her in my lap when she came home from the hospital. This moment was captured by Govind Chachu on Camera and my smile says it all. She was my new toy. Even today I call her my Maggie Darling.

When she was small probably around 5-6 years old, she fell very sick with jaundice and typhoid; this affected her health very badly. It is said the drugs given to her had various side effects and once she was back Pushpa Mummy became very possessive about her.

Her movements were restricted and her food habits were greatly curtailed, but one thing about Meghana was that she always kept smiling. She took up arts as a habit and is a good painter. Another memory with Meghana is the time we ended up in a rindle, but that story for some other time.

She took the lectures of Govind Chachu also very seriously, more than I ever did always topping her class and that is why she is now a renowned Gynaecologist having a flourishing practice but for me she is and shall always remain my Maggie Darling.

She was Govind Chachu's muse, his model as she was and is still very pretty with a very photogenic face.

She has worked very hard to reach the position she has reached. Her husband Divyagyan is a renowned Ophthalmologist and she also had a love marriage. Divya is a great guy, always smiling and helping people around, doing charity here and there. They have two daughters' identical twins Heer and Himani whom I still cannot differentiate.

Shweta my Sister, like I have said was a Tom Boy. Always ready for a fight, even today. She can also start crying at the drop of a hat. She was always a rebel, wanting to break the mould, unlike me. She was like me never serious in studies, but because she wanted to break out. She put in an extra effort during her 12th and managed to get herself into a renowned Hotel Management Institute in Manipal and was the first female to move to a hostel far away from home.

My father like I have said was modern and conservative at the same time. He encouraged Shweta to move out and study but at the same time, after a couple of drinks regretted sending her away. But that was Daddy being Daddy.

Shweta completed her internship in Taj Lake End in Udaipur, and started working in Leela Mumbai where she met Nand her future husband. Shweta's courtship was also one crazy one. She one time pulled up a bill of close to 28,000 on STD calls to Nand when he was in Calicut, his home town. It is this time she confided in us that she was seeing Nand. I had a hint, but I did not push Shweta to confide in me till she wanted to.

Since I was protective about Shweta, I remember talking to Daddy and Mummy and asking them to allow me to first meet Nand and understand how serious they are about each other. Once I met Nand, I liked him and since both of them wanted to settle down in life with each other, I spoke to my parents and the way I convinced them was simple. I said "Shweta is a very head strong person and if we do not do things her way, believe me she will rebel. It is best that Shweta decides her own future as only then she will work hard to make it work".

Luckily for me those words worked and also more luckily for me, I was proved right. Shweta and Nand are now happily married for close to 15 years with 2 beautiful kids Yutika and my little pocket dynamite Dev. Shweta is now a successful professional working in a big MNC and Nand is a successful Project Head in another MNC.

Nand is now more close to my father than I am and proof of this is that my father never offered me a drink but he did offer a drink to Nand, not that I would have taken it if he had offered.

Now comes the turn of Yash, Jagdish Papa's youngest and the most mischievous of us all. His dimpled smile and innocent eyes were to die for.

He was always up to something and because of his smile he could get away with anything and still does.

He was one inquisitive kid. Give him a fan and he shall put his hand in it, make him sit on a cycle and he shall put his leg inside. The incidences with Yash were probably our fault as we as a family had failed to understand how naughty a kid Yash was and still is, in spite of the early warnings.

As a child Yash was not scared of anything. Throw him in the air and he would laugh, put him on the edge of the bed and he would jump, signs which were clear but we unheeded it. If we had noticed it, I would also have been saved from 14 injections in my stomach. What a story it is.

I was probably around 11-12 years old and our school had just finished. Our tickets to Udaipur were booked and we were to leave after a couple of days. It was a Sunday and as usual after finishing my food, I decided to go out to play. I had a habit of just jumping from our boundary wall into the society garden and that is what I did.

However, as soon as I landed in the garden, I came face to face with a black dog with white patches. I did not pay any attention as wild dogs in our society were very common. I started walking away, but the dog started to follow me. I quickened my speed but immediately the dog jumped on me. Luckily I managed to move away and ran from there.

Good thing was that the dog did not follow me. I immediately ran to the watchmen of the society and told him of the wild dog. He with his stick in one hand said, he will take care.

I returned after playing an hour at my friend's house, but since I was scared I decided to ask the watchmen to walk me back to my house.

While we were walking back, the scene which I saw was both terrifying and funny. Yash barely 3 feet tall, in his vest and shorts holding a stick in his hand was standing in front of the same dog who had attacked me earlier. Yash probably thought it was a toy and wanted to play with it, but this play costed me dearly, as for some strange reason instead of getting scared I ran towards Yash and picked him up in my arms.

As soon as I had Yash in my arms, the dog decided to jump on us and I instantly put my hands out to push the dogs away, but what luck, my hand just went inside the dog's mouth and he as any dog would, just bit it.

Luckily for me the watchmen also ran along with me and managed to hit the dog and push him away from me and Yash and took me and Yash home, but by this time the damage was done, my 14 injections in my stomach were secured along with two holes, through and through on my right hand. With my bleeding hand, my parents took me to our family doctor who resided in our society itself to patch me up. After patching me up, the doctor gave a letter to my parents to go to the Municipal Hospital the next day to get my 14 Rabies shots.

What happened at the Municipal Hospital next was just hilarious. My mother took me to the hospital the next day and we were sitting outside the doctors chambers waiting for our turn and hold be hold, what I see, my best friend Ajay walking in with his mother who was also a doctor. The funniest thing had happened, apart from the dog having bitten me, he had also bitten Ajay earlier on the same day and his bite was on his backside as the dog bit him when he was running away.

When the doctor saw both of us, he just reached for his injections and asked "Who First?" The needle was a good 2-3 inches long as it had to be given through the stomach and seeing it, both me, and Ajay just panicked. Me, and Ajay both started running around the doctors chambers screaming "Pehla Woh, Pehla Woh", "He First, He First", Finally we agreed on the age formulae and since Ajay was 11 months elder to me, he went first.

Those next 14 days were painful ones. The stomach used to swell up after the injection and the pain used to last a good couple of hours. The dog bite instance gave me my Dog Phobia. I am shit scared of dogs even today and therefore my poor kids can't have a pet in their house.

Yash probably does not remember any of these instances of his naughtiness, but today when I see him playing and handling his 3 kids (Kaavya, Palak and Rajat), it looks to me like Yash is trying to pass on his naughtiness to his kids and Vijeta his wife is struggling to keep tabs on it.

His desire to experiment, he has taken to a logical level. Today he experiments with newer products mixing, designing and packaging them. He has become a successful entrepreneur in the food industry and he is on his way to create his own legacy

The only other cousins who were born before we moved from Chembur were Neha and Niti who were Raj Didi and Madan

Jijajee's daughters. Neha was a very cute kid. She had dimples on her chin and a beautiful smile. She was the first kid whom I actually started to take care off as a guardian and after her I was always the Big Brother for the rest of the siblings.

Neha visited us back a good 15 years later, while Niti came back to India a further 4 years later. Bianca was born abroad and the first time I saw her was when she was around 10 years old. Now when I look at Neha, all married with twins it feels so nostalgic. Hopefully, Niti shall be the next to get married followed by Bianca.

Ashok Chachu's kid Karan and Sona Didi's kid Shashank were born just a couple of months apart. Ashok Chachu and Vandana Chachi had Karan during their final year MD and since their final exams were coming up, Badi Mami, my Father and Mother got Karan home to us in Vashi. Karan was our little toy, we kids once back from school would just sit around him playing with him. I nicknamed Karan as Kanu Lal and have been calling him that ever since. Tanya, Tinu Darling as I called her was Ashok Chachu and Vandana Chachi's Daughter. The cutest kid I have ever seen.

I could spend hours taking care of my Tinu Darling and I did. Once the hospital was operational, and Chachu and Chachi were busy with running it, Tinu was with us as we stayed on the top floor of the hospital. She was very possessive about me and when I got married, initially she did not like Meeta much, but soon she accepted Meeta.

Karan did his Engineering from Vashi and his Masters from the US and married Nisha in a destination wedding in Goa.

Currently as I sit writing this, Karan is stuck in US along with Nisha, waiting to come back and start a new life in India. Tina married the love of her life Anatole (A Frenchmen) who she met in LA while doing her course of Photography and is now busy settling in US.

Shashank and Shivek were two kids with whom also I share a special bond. They call me Anu Mama as Sona Didi ties Rakhi to me. During my college days, Goa was my preferred destination as Sona Didi and Satish Jijajee had shifted there and started a fishing business and I was always welcome to their house.

Every college break I would take a bus from Mumbai to Goa and spend at least one week there. It is here that I developed my love for fish. Evening walks with Shashank and Shivek on the beach, playing with them when they returned from school was how I spent my days in Goa. Shashank married Lebina and they have a cute one year old son. Shivek is working with his father and hopefully shall get married soon.

Rohin and Rahul are two cousins whom I have spent the least amount of time with as they were born in US and have lived their whole life there. We have caught up many times but I would have liked to have spent more time with them. Rohin is now studying to become a medical professional, while Rahul is trying to find his steps in the world. Rohin is the quieter of the two, while Rahul is the Mission Impossible Tom Cruise type, always up to something. The good news is that Rohin has just got engaged and hopefully my next trip to US shall be for his wedding.

From my cousins on my Mother's side, it was Vipra and Ashish I have spent the maximum time with. Vipra is one brainy kid. She is the first of my cousins who has done a PHD and is now Dr. Vipra; she is now well settled in Singapore. Ashish followed in Ravi Mama's footsteps and became a CA and also did his MBA from IIM Bangalore and now is a successful banker. Ravi Mama would have been very proud of both of his kids and with the success they have achieved.

Apart from Tina the next kid I have spent max time taking care of, is Ashish. The stories of Ashish's tantrums are tales for some other time. Vipra on the other hand was the quite one but the story of we having forgotten her at a Restaurant is just hilarious. Ashish is now married to Pallavi and looking at him all settled in life makes me feel very proud of him.

Mini and Gini were two cousins of mine whom we met up when we travelled to Udaipur. With Mini, Gini and Shweta, it was always tea parties with toy tea sets. Lata Masi had Dhruv quite late and he was one chubby kid, but like Rohin and Rahul we caught up only a few times. Mini is now happily married to a cousin of mine with two lovely kids a boy and a girl while Gini too is married with a son who is just a few months old while I am writing this.

Mudit, who we also called Goldie, moved out of India when he was around 3 years old while Khushi was born outside India. Like Dhruv, I spent very little time with Mudit and Khushi. Mudit is one smart guy now, totally resembles Sonu Mama while Khushi has gone on Bobby Mami.

From my interactions with my cousins, one thing I am quite sure of, there is something in our genes which connects us. We might not meet for years, but when we meet it feels we were never apart.

I am closest to my sister as any brother would be, but we are totally different. How I look at life and how she looks at life is totally different too, this in spite of both of us going through almost the same set of experiences during our childhood.

But with my other cousins, there is a different connection, I am their eldest cousin but I am not their friend in the classical context that you would think. I am more of a cousin who they would easily give their kids whom they love, to be taken care of by.

Again a thought might have come to you, why I am making you read about my cousins. What is so great about them and what is so great about my interaction with them.

Why you need to know your sister or brother or cousins well is because it is they who are the ones who first understand you as a person. They are the first ones to know you inside out.

If you feel you are a friendly extrovert person and if your sister, brother and cousins cannot open up to you, you can safely assume you are not. Similarly if you think you are always a helpful guy and if your sister, brother or cousins feel they cannot ask for your guidance and help, then again you can safely assume you are not.

Your Siblings and Cousins are the true mirrors in whose eyes and behaviour you will find out, who you really are.

Your Siblings might be your mirror but you can always be influenced by them as well, as I was,

- From my Maggie Darling, how to keep smiling

- From Shweta, be a rebel but have a cause

- From Yash, Be careful

- From All My Cousins, Acceptance for who I am

If I have to describe in a few words the relationship I share with my sister and cousins, then those words shall be,

'You are the Ones,

Who gave me all my first memories

My first memories of,

What it meant to love someone

My first memories of,

What it meant to fight someone

My First memories of,

What it meant to care for someone

It is in these memories

I got my first,

My First Basket of Smile

My First True Memories of Life'

Chapter 5 - My Childhood Friends and My First School

Ajay, who shared the dog incidence with me, was my best friend growing up. The others in our group were Rajesh who was a couple of years elder to me and Rajiv who was Ajay's age who joined us later.

Ajay was a Christian and was the youngest child in his family. He had two elder brothers and an elder sister. His house was also a crazy one as Ajay's elders were a good 10 years elder to him. His eldest brother was into the business of importing bikes from abroad and selling them in India. In those days I had seen a 1000 cc Ninja Honda bike and had the experience of sitting on it. Although, I was only 8-10 years old at that time, this is one experience which I cannot forget.

Most of the time it was just me and Ajay who used to play together. Cricket was all about 12 balls of bowling and 12 balls of batting and seeing who scored more boundaries and took more wickets and football was all about taking penalties, seeing who scored more goals and who saved more.

Ajay had a very strange fetish of catching live crabs during the rainy season. The well at the entrance of the society had a drainage system which during the rainy season used to overflow with crabs popping up here and there. Ajay was not scared of them, as they ate them in their house, but I was scared of them, but with Ajay's instigation I would also enter the drains and try and catch them as his wingman and always ended up getting bitten by them.

My mom used to give me and Ajay a good scolding each time she caught us catching crabs in the drains, but for us this was an adventure which we could not let go off.

Rajesh, the other member of our group was a couple of years elder to me. His parents were very protective of him being the only son and would not allow him to play out much. His father owned an old fiat which was called a Ducker fiat in those days, shape similar to the Herbie car. It was always unlocked as the engine had given up but Rajesh's father would not sell it cheap, so it remained in his garage at least till the time I lived in Chembur.

Rajesh's bungalow had a big tiled play area where we used to play Badminton. Also we kids managed to arrange a table for playing table tennis which we kept in Rajesh's garage next to his fiat.

Rajiv was the last to enter our group. He moved into our adjacent society when I was around 10 years old. The first thing about Rajiv was his ears, they were big, like the ones Aamir Khan had in PK. Rajiv's father was a very strict guy and I do not recollect seeing him smiling even once. His mother was cute and allowed us to play in their house regularly. It was Rajiv who introduced me to my first intelligent game which I ever played which was Name, Place, Animal and Thing.

There were many other kids in the society whom I used to play with, but my special friends were only Ajay, Rajesh and Rajiv.

Apart from the fun time and fun memories, there are unpleasant ones as well. One of them being how one of our neighbourhood bullies would use his dogs to frighten us, especially me as my dog incident had happened and he used to rag us and make us do strange unpleasant things from a kid's perspective.

But luckily for me, my happy memories far exceeded these unpleasant one.

My first School, OLPS was an only boy's convent school. We had a father as a principal and my memories of OLPS pertain to our morning assembly prayers, the father coming around the school to check our uniforms and nails, playing football during our PT period, four corners during recess, buying and eating samosas, vada pav and 5-10 paisa candies from the canteen. We used to walk to our school as it was only a 10 minutes distance from our society. Another important routine while returning from school was playing at Diamond Garden, the public park which came between our society and school. Not a single day went by, when we did not visit that garden.

I do not have much recollection of any of my teachers in school; except for Dubey Sir our Hindi teacher and our English Teacher. Why I remember Dubey Sir, is because the kids in school had a song for him, "Neeche Pan Ki Dukan, Upar Dubey Ka Makan" (A Pan Shop Below and Dubey House on Top) as he had a habit for eating pan and his mouth was always red in colour due to the pan he ate. Don't ask why I remember my English Teacher.

Another memory of my school days was the vaccinations days where all of us kids were supposed to take our vaccination shots. You should have seen us kids after our shots, each kid holding his arms trying desperately not to cry. Another thing which OLPS used to do was organize movies for children day celebrations and take us all to Natraj Cinema and make us watch patriotic films at special screenings.

Not all memories about OLPS however are good ones. OLPS days did give me my stage fear along with shaping me as an introvert to a large extent.

It was our schools annual day and I was probably in 3rd grade when I got my stage fright fear going. A play was arranged where we were representing our freedom struggle days. I being a very fair kid was given the role of Bharat Mata. During practice, since there was no costume I did not realize what I would look like. All I knew was that I would have to come at the end of the play with an Indian flag in my hand and everyone would start clapping, simple.

But come Annual Day, my mother came along with me and dressed me up, made me wear a white saree and a wig with long hair, a big Bindi on my forehead and a crown on my head. It was now that I panicked. My worst fears were realized after the play was over, from the very next day in school and during the rest of the year, everyone in school started calling me Mata and my friend circle in school shrank.

Another issue in OLPS was that each year we were shuffled around in different classes and every year we were supposed to interact with a newer group of kids and that part was becoming difficult for me. After this I have always tried to avoid coming in the frontline of anything. Even today, you will find me at the other end of every party.

The time spent with my friends in Chembur and my experiences in OLPS were important in their own regard as they further helped shape me as to what I would become especially the time spent with Ajay playing football.

My Belief System picked up the following things from my experiences with my Childhood Friends and First School,

- From My Childhood Friends, Crabs and dogs are good but they bite, and practice makes you perfect (Stopping Goals)

- From Rajiv, there are intelligent games in the world and there is no harm trying newer things, you don't know what you might like

- From School, how to become an Introvert and what one needs to do to ensure one can survive happily in a group especially if you are introvert and that is become invisible but be present.

The words that describe my childhood days are,

'Bachpan Ke Woh Din

Kaun Bhool Sakta Hain

Yadein Woh Aisi Hain

Joh Zindagi Bhar Sath Rahengi

Mar Bhi Gaye Toh, Upar Jaa Kar Bhi

Kambhakath Hume Hasati Rahengi'

The above lines when translated in English Mean,

'Who can forgot, one's childhood,

They are the memories which shall remain with you for ever,

Even if you die, they shall come with you after your death,

To keep you Smiling after death'

Chapter 6 - My Core Group of Friends

The time I moved from Chembur to Vashi at the age of 14, I thought I would not survive without my society friends and we promised to stay in touch, but somehow we could not. I still remember them but I have not spoken to any of them since the day I left Chembur, in fact I have not entered my Chembur society since I left it. I found Rajiv on Facebook but have not chatted up with him still.

The next set of good friends I made in Vashi was Goldie and Manoj, who lived in the same building that I moved into from Chembur. Goldie like Ajay was a year elder to me while Manoj was my age. Goldie was a techno geek. He had computer games at his residence in 1989 and I remember playing endless hours of games at his house. Manoj was a huge bulky guy and we called him our body guard. We named our group after seeing the film Goonies, the Gooeezz. Goldie was also big time into hearing English songs and introduced me to the Pet Shop Boys, Michel Jackson and Madonna.

Till moving to Vashi, I had never heard or seen any of them and my life was surrounded by Mohd Rafi, Kishore Kumar, Lata Mangeshkar, Asha Bhosale, Mukesh and Mana Dey. In Chembur it was only about playing cricket, football. Badminton, table tennis and watching movies and DD Serials but once I landed up in Vashi, my world changed.

The school, Sacred Heart High School was a 5 minute walk from our society and that is why it was chosen. I, Shweta, Meghana and Yash all joined that school in the year 1989. I joined this school in my 9th grade.

It was Goldie who took the initiative to befriend us kids and introduces us to every kid in the society. He was and still is a very jovial person and he had one of the best walks I had seen and his style of adjusting his turban was just too good.

Manoj on the other hand was a big bully but with a soft heart. He had a moustache and looked much older than his age. He too was a big movie buff like me. I remember an incidence when he instigated me to go along with him to a matinee show at one of the two theatres in Navi Mumbai. It was a horror film on the lines of Ramsay Brothers. We bought the tickets and sat down with our popcorn. Once the film started within 10 minutes we realized this movie was altogether something else. I remember very clearly looking at Manoj and seeing the horror in his eyes than on the screen. I quietly stood up, pinched Manoj and we both walked out of the theatre within 15 minutes of the show starting. Once out we had a big laugh on what we had gone through.

It was with Goldie and Manoj that I experienced a lot of firsts as well. The experience included my first train ride to VT to watch an English film in a theatre in town, shopping on Fashion Street and having my first plate of Pav Bhaji with them.

Once I left my society in Vashi I never looked back and neither maintained contacts with Goldie, Manoj and the rest of the friends as it happened with my previous buddies Ajay, Rajiv and Rajesh.

Adjusting to Vashi was easy thanks to Goldie and my friends there, but when it came to "Sacred Heart", it was initially tough as I was coming from an all boy's school and my interactions with girls were limited to my sisters and a few friends of my sisters in Chembur.

On the first day of school itself I realized thanks to my cocooned life in Chembur, I could not speak with girls. I being a new entrant, the class teacher introduced me and since all front benches were occupied, I was made to sit in the last row. As I always loved to sit behind in class, I happily went across and sat down. Another reason for me being happy was that all the girls were sitting in the front few rows.

It was later that I realized, that scholars are made to sit ahead and since girls in our class were all brilliant they sat in front and the mischievous one's who were mostly boys, were made to sit behind as per the Sacred Heart hierarchy. Because I sat at the back of the class and owing to the school's hierarchy standards, my first sets of friends were the most mischievous ones, but I enjoyed their company.

My days in Sacred Heart facilitated to get my name in the newspapers, not once but twice, once in school and second time when I was in college. How I got my name there is a very interesting story. It started in my first Physical Training period. We had a PT teacher called Benedict. He was our PT teacher but was not much of a sports person.

Since I was a new kid in class, he made me stand up and asked me a simple question "What all outdoor games did I play?" I said "Football" instinctively. He then followed it up with a second question "What Position?" Here I was dumb folded. I played football but for me football was playing penalties with Ajay and kicking around the ball in the OLPS school ground.

I said "Sir, I don't understand" to which Benedict Sir replied "Forward, Mid Field or Defence". I after a second replied "Forward", thinking since Football was all about scoring goals, forward sounded just right. Immediately Benedict said "Report for trials on this coming Saturday Morning 8:00 am". I said "OK".

Not knowing what I was getting into, I reached the grounds at 8:00 am sharp in my comfortable ankle high sport shoes. My fellow players looked at me and started laughing. Luckily the captain of the team Nimesh, came up to me and said, you need to buy special shoes for football and they are available at a local shop in Sector 17 and when you come for the next practice buy them and come.

My trials with the team were hopeless. I was very bad at being a Centre Forward but since there were only a few of us, I was retained in the team as an extra. During one practice session, our team's regular goalkeeper got injured, since there was no other substitute, Benedict Sir asked me to go and stand under the goal post, while the rest of the players tried to kick the ball towards the goal.

Now came the part for me to shine, thanks to my days playing with Ajay in Chembur. Since this was a one on one system similar to penalties, I excelled. I did not allow a single goal in and everyone looked at me in shock. From that day onwards, I was the No 1 Goalkeeper of Sacred Heart High School.

Another shining moment came when our team defeated our enemies 'Father Agnel High School' for the first time in football. Both teams had not scored a single goal during the regular time hence, the match was supposed to be decided on penalties. The saves I made during the penalty shoot-out were extraordinary. Diving left right and centre I saved all penalties leading the team to victory and I was upheld as the Hero.

The next day in school during assembly my name was read out by the principal and all of a sudden, every kid in school knew my name, from a 'Nobody' I became a 'Somebody'. But I did not enjoy this adulation much as this meant I was in the limelight. Even though I became popular, my friend circle remained the back benchers.

Our team went across to the Divisional Play offs thanks to our victory and for the first time in my life I travelled without my family, our entire football team travelled to Bhusawal to play Inter Division Matches for the under 16 Subroto Cup. The train trip was fun with everyone laughing and just enjoying themselves.

When we landed in Bhusawal, we were put up at the stadium itself. Mattresses were given to us along with a bedsheet and blanket and bathrooms were open air ones. On the match day, to our surprise, we were told we had got a "bye" in our first round as the 4th team could not come and we were straight through to the finals.

The other semi-final was to happen between a Local Bhusawal school and Bhusawal Military School. The Bhusawal Military

School kids were smart, strong kids in their crew cut hair but the team opposite them comprised of men and not kids. To our surprise the organizers did not take objection to the fact that some of the players of the Local Bhusawal School were clearly overage. A few even had bikes and drove cars when they reached the ground to play.

But as it is said 'In India Anything Can Happen'. Driving licences are given to kids although legal age of license issue is 18 years, but it happens only in India. After this nothing unexpected happened. Bhusawal Military School lost 3-0 while we lost the final 4-0.

Everybody in school now knew me and I started feeling as if I was invincible. I started practicing less and thought no one can defeat me and come next year, we lost our very first match to Father Agnel due to a stupid error on my part, from a hero to a zero in one year itself. Luckily for me my team mates stood with me.

But how did I get my name in the papers?

My football story did not end with this loss to Father Agnel; it just took a turn for the better. Since we were out of the main Subroto Cup, our coach put our schools name in the Maharashtra Inter School Rural Games. During one of our training sessions, I got myself a small crack on my left foot and my leg had swollen up and low and behold, within a day of me getting hit on my leg, we received a message that our Inter school matches would be held the next week.

Our half year semester exams were to be held a day after the matches and most of our team mate's parents objected to it. My family too objected to it on two fronts, one exam and second my swollen foot. But a few of my friends were some desperate blokes. In spite of all the objections, it was decided within our team meeting that we shall go for the matches. It was agreed we shall meet at Mankhurd Railway Station and from there we shall go to Kurla and then onwards to Ambernath.

I convinced my parents that I will go with my team mates but shall not play and anyway my parents by now knew I was not interested in studies, so they let me go. It was 6 am in the morning when I reached Mankhurd, there I saw a couple of my team mates. We waited for some time for the others and thought we had missed them and probably the others had taken the earlier train and reached Kurla so we also took the next train and reached Kurla.

We waited at Kurla for around 15 minutes and a total of 7 including me landed up there. The remaining 7 probably did not get their parents to allow them.

Sitting at Kurla station we had two options, one go back home and two proceed to Ambernath and play with all 7 including me, as the minimum count for a team to be eligible to play was 7. We all agreed what the hell!, we had permission to bunk school and we were already half way to the ground, we shall go across and play with the strength of 7 with me sitting pretty under the goal post doing nothing.

We landed up at the ground and when we informed the organizers we were 7, they asked us are we sure we want to play and we said yes and they put our match first. Here we were

7 against 11; even the other team had a laugh at us. Before the match started, we just had a quite word amongst us and said to each other, let us enjoy ourselves as we had nothing to lose.

During the match something strange happened, I played my best games, saved a couple of penalties, did a few good blocks, we lost badly but we also managed to score a couple of goals, Ronald our Centre Forward also had a great game with the couple of goals he scored.

Even the opposite team appreciated the challenge we put up. After the game, when we were cleaning up, the referee of the game came across to our side and took down my and Ronald's name. We returned back and forgot all about our names being put down by the referee. But again I was in for a surprise. After around 15 days, we received a letter from Thane Regional Football board stating Anup and Ronald have been selected to be part of the Thane District Team in the Inter District Tournament.

The Inter District Tournament, were to be conducted in Kolhapur and we took a road trip. I, Ronald and Benedict Sir our PT Teacher took a bus all the way to Kolhapur. In Kolhapur our team was put up at the Kolhapur Stadium with similar arrangements of sleeping on the floor and stinking toilets as in Bhusawal. In Kolhapur our Thane Team won our first match, but lost the second one, but again my performance was appreciated. We returned back immediately the same night after we lost the match.

Again all was forgotten till another letter was received by the school a month later stating that I was selected to be a part of the Maharashtra Football Team to take part in the All India

Rural Games to be held in Lucknow. Immediately on this news reaching the principal's office, there was an announcement on the school speaker system, stating Anup Gawdi to report to the principal's office.

Hearing my name, I got scared but when the principal gave me the good news, it was fantastic. I was the first kid to be selected from the school for anything and therefore, my school took it upon themselves to call a local reporter and have my name put across in the Local Navi Mumbai newspaper. This is how I got my name in the newspaper for the first time.

My trip to Lucknow for the Nationals was a story in itself. The Nationals were to take place 20 days before our 10th Board exams and like any parent whose child is in 10th, my parents also raised concerns.

The school however convinced my parents that if I participated in the National Games, I would get extra credit for the same in my 10th board exams. Anyways, I was not a great kid in studies and my parents knew it, so getting anything extra they thought would be great for me and allowed me to go.

However, the journey to Lucknow would not be easy, The Maharashtra Sports federation was only sponsoring my ticket and any companion who had to come with me would need to bear their own expenses. Our school was a stingy one, but since I was going alone they agreed to allow me to be accompanied by Benedict Sir to Nagpur where the rest of players from all over Maharashtra would assemble and then together go to Lucknow.

There Benedict Sir was to discuss with the federation and ensure I would get escorted back to Mumbai. The federation agreed to ensure I reach Mumbai safely and accordingly Benedict Sir left me and went back to Mumbai. In Lucknow we were put up again in a Stadium with mattresses to sleep on the floor and stinking toilets to use.

Our first match was against Bengal the defending champions. On reaching the ground, what do we see, the Bengal team players looked huge, no way were they Under 16 years of age as was mandated. They had huge builds with beards and moustaches but like I have said previously in India anything can happen. We were no saints either, in our team also I was the youngest and I was barely underage. We lost the game to Bengal with a 2-0 score line. Immediately the same night, we left for Nagpur.

On reaching Nagpur another surprise awaited me. I was made to sign a voucher stating that I had received an allowance of Rs 900, while in actual I received only 200 and an unreserved train ticket to Mumbai. Like I said anything can happen in India.

When I enquired who would be accompanying me to Mumbai, my Maharashtra team coach said you need to do it on your own, their responsibility ends here. Here I was all of 16 years of age, all by myself on Nagpur Railway Station without a slightest clue of anything. I had never been alone in my entire life so travelling alone was unheard of for me and here I was supposed to make a journey all the way from Nagpur to Mumbai by train and then from Mumbai Central Station to Mankhurd by train again to Vashi by bus.

But somehow I gathered courage within me and decided to speak to a Coolie at the platform and asked him how I should get from Nagpur to Mumbai on the ticket I had. He looked at my ticket and told me there is the Geetanjali Express which is coming to this platform and since the journey from Nagpur to Mumbai is a day one, I could try entering the second class sleeper compartment if the seats are empty. Once the train came, I entered the Sleeper class compartment and took up berth in one of the upper berths, not realising that just because the upper berth was empty it does not mean it is free.

Luckily for me since I was wearing the Maharashtra Jersey, the rest of passengers around me, allowed me to occupy that upper berth and did not disturb me. Also there was no Ticket Collector who came around inspecting and therefore I was saved.

The 15 hours journey from Nagpur to Mumbai I completed with 1/5 kg of grapes which I picked up from one of the stations and 1 litre of bottled water.

It was thanks to Football that I also got an opportunity to visit the police station next to my house. Our ground where we practiced was adjacent to NBSA, a sports club and because our control on our kicks was not that great, our ball used to invariably land up in the parking lot of NBSA. Probably because of one of our kicks landing on someone important or a car belonging to some VIP, we had a couple of constables coming across to our ground and rounding us up and taking us to the police station. Here we were these 15 year old kids, sitting inside a police station waiting for the Inspector to come to put us behind bars.

Luckily, the inspector was a good person who after giving us a warning let us all go. After coming out, we started calling ourselves the Tadi Pars (outcast) as after that we avoided playing football at the ground and even if we played we used the other end of the field.

Since my Nationals in Lucknow were only 20 days prior to the Board Exams, my mother allowed me to go only on the condition that I study first and get myself ready for the boards. This instigation I think worked wonders, as when the Boards results were handed over to me by the Principal, her words which I still cannot forgot were "This is totally unexpected". I had scored a distinction for the first time in my life and my percentage was 80.55% and needless to say my parents and everyone at home were thrilled.

With my sports credentials and results I was able to get admission to one of the finest Commerce Colleges of Mumbai, Ramniranjan Anandilal Podar College of Commerce and Economics. Commerce I choose for 2 reasons, one Ravi Mama and two my friends.

Coming to my friends, it was in Sacred Heart and Vashi where I got my core group of friends and what characters they were, each one better than the other. So where do I start.

Let's start with Udit, as he was one of the instigators for me to take up Commerce along with Sunil. Udit was the most hairy kid in the class. He also loved to be surrounded with girls and played most of the times with them, whether it was Jolly – Jolly or Hopingo Batingo. Jolly – Jolly was a game, wherein one needs to always have a small dot made with a pen called a jolly on your hand, anytime any kid can come across, show you his jolly and ask to see your jolly and if you don't have the jolly, you are supposed to get a nice whack on your back. Hopingo – Batingo was also something similar. In the middle of a class break invariably you would hear a cry of a girl and when you looked in the direction of the girl you will see Udit there and the cry was due to the whack the poor girl had got from Udit.

With Udit you could not have a dull moment as he was always up to something or the other. He was also the most accident prone. The first time I visited Udit at his house was when we were told in school that Udit has had a fracture and he cannot come to school. Since he stayed just a couple of minutes from the school, it was decided that after school we shall visit him and enquire about his health.

When we reached his house, we could not hold back our laughter. Here was Udit with both his arms in plaster from his fingers to his shoulder. He had managed to fracture not one but both his hands from the fall from the first floor of his house while flying kites.

Udit also had a large appetite and would eat almost anything. He could mix Thump Up with Samber and drink it; he could eat cake with red chillies. Give him any weird combination and he will try it. He also had a very peculiar habit of smelling everything. He initially did not drink, but enjoyed smelling the liquor and now has progressed to drinking Cocktails and Wines.

We were 100% sure that Udit would have a love marriage, but strangely he went in for an arranged one. One thing about Udit's family comprising of his mother and elder brother Umang was the strength they exhibited when Udit lost his father when he was in 10th standard. All of them stuck together and managed to take care of each other. Today, Udit is well settled as a CIO with a big MNC with a loving wife Nidhi and 2 lovely children Unnati and Udyan.

The next person in my group was Sunil, Sunny Boy as I call him. He and his sister Rakhi who later became my sister as well were one group of kids who were the most protected by their parents.

With Sunil everything was about what his mother said, from what one can and one cannot do, from what one can and one cannot eat.

Rakhi was 11 months younger than Sunil, but since Sunil's parents were very protective, they decided to put Sunil and Rakhi in the same grade. In those days, age eligibility was not that a serious issue and school usually allowed it as long as the fees were paid.

Rakhi although younger was the bolder of the two, while Sunil was a pure Mama's Boy. He was a very skinny kid as well and his ambition right up to the time he did his graduation was put on weight.

To put on weight he tried eating eggs, chicken and everything else. To put on weight he also tried to go to the gym and even started drinking beer as he thought he would get a beer belly, but to no avail. Once he got married, he achieved his goal of putting on weight and now he has hit the gym again but this time to get it off.

Another regret he had was in spite of him studying very hard all through the 10th and me playing all through my 10th, he just was one mark ahead of me and I got admission to Podar because of my sports quota while he could not. Remember the scene from '3 Idiots' when the results were announced, that is what Sunil felt. Sunil after 12th joined me in Podar but that is another story for some other time.

Sunil also had an unpleasant habit of disregarding people around him. If Sunil gets up early, instead of being quiet and letting others sleep, he would ensure everyone else also gets up, not directly waking them but by making enough noise that others woke up.

Another trait of Sunil is that he loves socializing, he is a party animal. For a party he shall forget his best friends as well, as he did with me once, for which he got one big kick on his backside which he remembers till date. Sunil tried his hands in different things from setting up a garments factory to doing Law after B.com.

Now he is a successful property lawyer and has ventured into construction with a loving wife Radhika and two lovely daughters Dia and Hitika.

The next in our group was Purvesh, Puri for me; he like me was a late entrant to Sacred Heart School and was the youngest of 3 brothers. He had come from a Boarding School in Kodaikanal and joined Sacred Heart in 8th grade. With Purvesh the thing you shall notice when you meet him is that he tries to be funny but actually he is not.

Another thing about Purvesh is his appetite. My mother experienced his appetite first hand, when one day she invited my friends to lunch at our place. We all finished up early but my mother kept on making chapatti's for Purvesh and Purvesh kept on eating them, after around 19 chapatti's my mother literally came out of the kitchen and said, "All atta finished, now pack up you kids". Even today my mother recounts Purvesh as the kid who ate 19 chapattis and my father remembers Purvesh as the kid who broke his Cielo's gear box. Purvesh has done everything from trading in IT products to going to Dubai to sell military equipment's to working in the supply chain side of an E Commerce company.

He had an arranged marriage and the time in Goa when he left me and Sunil all alone to go to Vasanti's house in Calicut to be with her before his marriage, is one such incident we keep teasing him with. The relationship which he shares with his son Aryan is very beautiful.

Then we had Deepak. Deepak was a kid I met during my French Board paper. He sat in front of me and it was with his slight help, that I could pass my French exams with flying colours. Later we met again in a bus as we both got our admissions in Podar College of Economics.

Deepak was a quiet guy but from inside he was and still is very mischievous. You know a person who wants to try things in life, funny things but shall not express it but push you to push him to do it, that is Deepak. He is now well settled in Geneva and working with the UN with a lovely wife Renu and 2 lovely daughters.

Now we come to Chandan, CC (don't ask for the full form please) for us friends. He was Deepak's friend and since Deepak joined our gang, CC also joined our gang. Chandan had a philosophy in life, whoever is an idiot gets the best looking wife (the Hindi translation is the one he said) and rightly so, he got a very beautiful wife and his life goal was achieved, just kidding.

He and Deepak were the real scholars in our group, both toppers in CA. With CC you can always expect the unexpected. From drinking 700 ml of Chivas in one sip, to puking in his own house, to always trying anything new, one could count on CC to be one adventurous bloke.

His adventures sometimes required me to clean up as being the only guy who never drank or smoke, my duty at times was to ensure things are cleaned up after the party is over and ensuring there is no trace left for the parents to see the next day. Today CC is well settled in Bahrain and heading a PE firm, with a lovely wife and two children, one daughter and one son.

Aditya, we also met in Podar, was a huge fellow but with one of the sweetest smiles. His father was a chairman of a large PSU and thanks to his father being in the PSU, we got to enjoy the guest houses which the PSU had in Lonavala and Goa free of cost. No wonder the PSU went bust, just kidding.

Aditya, although very calm most of time, had a very wild temper and Sunil was at the receiving end of one such wild one.

We had gone to the PSU Guest house in Lonavala and Sunil being Sunil kept on insisting that we need to go to Fariyas (a 5 star hotel in Lonavala) to have coffee. He kept pestering Aditya to go and the scene when Aditya lost it was one funny one. Here was Sunil, all skinny with a waist of 24 Inches and chest of 30 and here was Aditya a full on beast having a chest of 44 inches, shouting back at Sunil saying "Tujhe Chalna Hai, Hain Na, Chal, Chal, Chal Main Leh Chalta Huin"(You want to go, Right, So Come, Come, Come, Lets Go Now).

I have never seen Sunil more scared as I saw him then. He was not expecting this reaction from Aditya. At the end we did go to Fariyas in one of our subsequent trips, but it was one lousy Coffee which we had there and Sunil himself admitted to it.

Aditya and his wife Pradnya after marriage shifted to Singapore but have now settled back in Vashi with a lovely daughter.

There was Samir, who we got to know through Deepak and CC as Samir lived in Deepak's building. Samir was not from our college as he pursued his civil engineering from Pen. He was short in height but was one hell of a fast bowler. Samir was a funny guy, with a dry sense of humour.

Like Purvesh, Samir has tried a lot of things in life. He did his civil engineering, but ended up managing his father's chemical factory. He moved from the chemical factory to setting up a Spa and finally to becoming a Builder in Manipur, one crazy life. He is now not well settled, with he being in Manipur during the lockdown and his wife Runa with his twins a boy and girl in Mumbai. One thing about Samir is that he can have a lot of beer, a lot I mean.

Then we had Avi, our Chachu as he was Deepak's elder brother and our advisor in chief. Avi taught our group of kids everything that was to be taught. Our bachelor's parties were not complete without the knowledge of our great Chachu. Our sessions at C-45, are legendary. C-45 was our place for get-together, for card parties, drinking parties, cooking parties, movie parties, you name it and we have partied there.

Avi was and is still is a very good cook. It was he who taught me the basics of cooking as well. Most of the bad habits which we have in the group had origins with Avi, but at the same time Avi is one person who even today ensures we all meet and catch up every now and then.

He is now a successful business man with a lovely wife Rajani and two lovely daughters, Disha and Navya.

With Avi you can always expect he saying something which he should not, like the time he called the waiter in the Restaurant "Kala Coat", to the incident of the Patiala Peg in Goa at my Didi's residence. But one thing about Avi is, what is there in his heart is there on his lips.

Chetan was one friend I got introduced to in Podar as he too was a sports person. Chetan along with Rupesh, Umesh, Ashraf, Faisal, Sandesh, Rahul, Tushar, Yogesh and others were my sporty gang from college.

Chetan joined our gang in Vashi when he moved to Vashi and started travelling with us. The instance of Chetan losing it at Appetite is one funny incidence. This incidence was also a lesson for our Gang that one should not drink on an empty stomach, because if you do, even one peg is just too many.

Chetan's father ran a Hotel in Dadar and Chetan also ventured into the Hotel industry. He worked in Uganda and Bahrain and has now returned back to Mumbai with his wife Madhuri who is an avid Marathoner and a lovely daughter.

We also had Rakesh with us. Rakesh was the son of a jeweller and we met him in Podar. Rakesh was the first of us to get married, immediately on completing his 12th and he turning 19.

His wedding at Hyderabad which we attended was one big party for us. From the train ride to Hyderabad, to the guest house where we were put up in, to the actual wedding, it was just great fun. It was at Rakesh's wedding that people enquired about me as well and Avi still makes fun that if I had agreed he could have made a cool 2 crores by selling me off.

The incidence of Rakesh at my Bachelor's party was just hilarious. "The mystery of the Poop in the middle of the Kitchen", is one mystery which till date is unsolved. Rakesh today is now a photographer for the stars in Hyderabad. He is well settled there with his wife Rakhi and 2 boys and a girl.

Ashutosh was another member of our Gang, but we lost him in FY B.com. By losing I do not mean dead, he is very much hale and hearty and living in Ahmedabad, by losing I mean, he moved to Ahmedabad with his family when we were in FY B.com.

Ashutosh was a good badminton player and decent in studies but for some insecurities which he developed, these insecurities put him into a different zone and it was best felt by his parents that for Ashutosh's betterment it would be good if they moved to Ahmedabad.

With Ashutosh and Rakesh there was one really funny incident which happened in Goa. Thanks to Aditya, we had gone to Goa for the very first time (we were in FYJC) and were staying at the PSU Guest House in Miramar Area. Being first time in Goa, it was like free beer everywhere.

It was probably our second day in Goa and Avi had stocked the fridge with various types of beers Mild, Strong, Very Strong. It was breakfast time and all of us were having our breakfast with Ashutosh and Rakesh sleeping, at least that is what we thought.

We must have just finished our breakfast when we heard Ashutosh and Rakesh laughing like crazy. We all went to the swing area and here there where these two idiots sitting on the swing, with each holding a Haywards 10000 bottle in their hands, laughing away to glory. Probably as soon as both of them had got up, they had decided on their own that instead of starting their day with a glass of milk they should start it with a bottle of beer. These idiots were totally tipsy. We tried our best to control them but they started enacting the scene of Gabbar and Samba from Sholay, pointing imaginary guns in our directions and shooting at us. Till today we refer to both Ashutosh and Rakesh as Gabbar and Samba.

After this trip Aditya never took us to any of the PSU Guest Houses as by now our reputation had reached Aditya's father.

Except for Ashutosh, the rest of us have been in touch even to this day and we regularly meet up with our families.

Apart from these guys there are others who for some reason or the other, I had lost touch with in course of my life, but have now connected with them again, thanks to our school's what's app group.

You will be asking me why no Girls in my list of friends. The answer is plain and simple; it was difficult for me to speak to girls when I was growing up. It is not that I totally could not speak to them, but being shy, my conversations with them was always to the point.

Girls with whom I could speak a little freely with were Rakhi (Sunil's Sister), Pooja, Rinku and Kuntal. Apart from them it is only now that I am able to speak to the girls from my school, thanks to the efforts of Joe and Ansley who have set up our school's What App group and keep organizing our get-togethers.

My life in Sacred Heart was also filled with various funny incidences and anecdotes, a few which I would like to share with you through these memoirs.

There was Tots, who was one crazy guy. He was an athlete, a 100 meter sprinter and a good one at that but at the same time I can safely say he had a screw loose as well.

He had set up a Chemistry Lab in his house as he said he loved Chemistry, not from a study point of view but a blowing up point of view. He used to smuggle chemicals from our school chemistry lab along with test tubes and other stuff and blow things up at home. The way he got caught was really funny.

One day he decided to steal some sulphur and to do so put the crystals in the pocket of his shorts and walked out of the lab. He probably forgot he had the crystals in his shorts and during PT when we were playing football in the morning heat, the crystals melted.

Here was Tots standing on the ground with his legs fully coloured up in the yellow sulphur liquid. What a lecture he received. But no amount of lectures could stray him from his path.

There was another incident, this time in the Biology Lab. During our 10th, in our Biology practical one of things we were supposed to do is look into the Microscope and try and identify different types of Amoeba. I clearly remember Tots coming up to us on the day of the practical's and telling us "Don't worry I have taken care, you do not need to even look into the microscope, just answer this". When we asked him how he was sure he calmly said 'Because I have the other slide in my pocket". He was one crazy guy.

Another incident of his craziness was when he broke his arm on the football field. Here we were panicking and there he was all smiling and laughing while looking at his broken hand, in fact he was playing with it and shouting out "Dekh Mera Hath Toot Gaya" (Look I have broken my hand).

There were many more funny instances like the one with Faisal and the Chemistry paper, the one with the leaked Hindi paper, the one with Me and my friends Sunil, Purvesh and Nair being called to the Principals office, the one with me being teased with a girl, so many of them, just so many.

Apart from these incidents, my trips with my friends were also just terrific. The trip to Vaishno Devi and Dalhousie when we were in FY B.com, the various trips to Lonavala and Goa, each filled with so much fun, laughter and fights as well. Each time we travelled as a group there was at least one incident which stood out.

Whether it was the electrical shorting incident in Avi's car or the time I slid my car into a drain on the National Highway or the time when Deepak and Sunil tried to offer a lift to a group of girls in Goa or the time I almost had hyperthermia while climbing to Vaishno Devi shrine or to the time my friends tried to befriend a group of girls in Dalhousie, so many of them, just so many.

Another incident which I want to share with you'll is the time after my 10th results, just before my college started when I received an invite from Maharashtra Sports Federation that a training camp for young footballers was being organized in Jalna and I needed to go there for a 7 day camp. Again my school said, I needed to make my own arrangements. Since no one from my family could come, I told my parents I shall travel alone. I had already experienced the Train journey from Nagpur to Mumbai alone, so I confidently said; Jalna was half the distance, so easy.

My parents reluctantly agreed and my father put me on a Luxury bus to Aurangabad. From Aurangabad I needed to take another local bus to Jalna. It was just an overnight journey, so again I thought it was easy. When we reached Aurangabad and exited the bus, to my horror, I realized that my bag had been offloaded at an earlier stop due to some confusion with another group of passengers who got off at that stop.

Here I was all alone in Aurangabad, with barely any money and no bag. I somehow managed to control my tears and went across to a pay booth to call my parents.

As is the standard practice with Indian parents, instead of comforting me, I received a blasting saying how careless I am. I was controlling my tears till then, but with the scolding I received, I could not hold them further. My father immediately instructed me to go back to the spot I had got down and take the next bus back to Mumbai.

As instructed I walked back to the final drop point and what I saw there finally got a smile to my face. An old man who had got off earlier, had come to handover my bag as he had realized the mistake. I called my father again and said, I had found my bag and I would be going ahead to Jalna.

At Jalna like all my previous trips with the Maharashtra Football Federation, we were put up at a school with bug ridden mattresses and torn bed sheets for company. Food at the school was always the same, for breakfast poha, for lunch dal, rice along with potato veg, and one banana in the evening and for dinner dal, rice along with potato veg. All 7 days. The camp however was good and I managed to better my skills as a keeper, which became helpful to me when I played football for my College and played in Mumbai's 2nd Division.

Like I said previously, my life took a full turn once I landed up in Vashi from Chembur. It is thanks to the move from Chembur to Vashi which resulted in me making such lovely friends and creating such lovely memories.

If it was not for this group of wonderful people I would not become what I have become and I would not have the memories which I always look back on when I am feeling down and immediately, the sad feelings are replaced by a sense of happiness.

I am sure in everyone's life there are these friends whom you cannot forget and just the mention of their names bring back happy memories and brings a big smile on your face and for that short duration of time makes you forgot all your problems, this my friends is my second solution for avoiding frustration entering into one's life. Also now you know why my Friends come in at No 2 in my priority listing.

I am also sure that these set of friends would have influenced your thinking and behaviour as well, like they did to me and what I have listed below as my learnings,

- The memories you make with your friends, your cousins and your elders always bring a smile to your face, so make as many as you can as who will definitely need them in the long life ahead

- From Goldie and Nimesh, I learnt that helping someone goes a long way in helping someone to become someone

- Never become scared when things don't go your way, you can panic but only for some time and then you can always come up with a solution

- Never be too overconfident about your abilities, Life has a way of getting you back to the ground

- When one door closes, another always opens up

- Seeing Udit and the problems faced by him so early in life probably made me more responsible about myself and feel how fortunate I am and also made me realise how not to behave with girls.

- With Sunny Boy, I realized so much about what to eat and what not to eat and what to eat with what and what one should not do while being a social animal and that is forgot friends while partying

- With Puri, I realized being quite is better than trying to crack a joke which is not funny and small size men can have huge appetite.

- With Deepak, I realized we can try and control our mischievous side but it sooner or later comes out.

- With CC I realized that you should be prepared for the unexpected when it comes to friends.

- With Avi, knowledge is the power.

- With Sammy, just hang in there and things will work out.

- With Chetan, just be yourself.

- With Adi use your smile to charm the ladies, just kidding. Adi was one quite guy and a terrific friend you can always count on.

- I also learnt an important lesson about India and that is, 'Anything Can Happen In India'

The words that describes my friends are,

'Yaar Woh Hote Hain,

Jinko Yaad Karte Hi

Aihsas Hota Hai

Kya Matlab Hai Khushi Ka

Kya Matlab Hai Zindagi Ka'

This in English translates into,

'Friends are those,

Whose memories bring a smile on your face

And make you realize what life is all about'

Chapter 7 - Meeta

To begin the next part of my journey into my belief system, it is important to take you to my college days. Like it is said a woman can make or break a person. Luckily, I found the woman who made me in R.A. Podar College of Commerce and Economics and this is the story of how I met her and what happened thereafter.

Everyone needs someone in his/her life which he/she can rely on 100% and that someone makes their life worth living and moving forward and for me that was Meeta.

My parents are an important and integral part of my life as I am sure your parents also are in your lives. But as per me, it is your spouse you share everything with and therefore he or she commands a different space in your life as it did with me in the case of Meeta.

Meeta was a jovial, fun loving girl, always up to some mischief with a gang of girls to match. She was quite popular with boys as well as was proved when she was crowned the Rose Queen in her first year of junior college. Probably what attracted me to her first time was her smile and the way she was full Bindass (Never Scared of Others), totally unlike me.

With Meeta one thing was sure, give her something to try for the first time and 10 times out of 10 she would try it. There was and there still is a great level of inquisitiveness in her. Tying her down during college days was just not possible. Wherever there was any fun thing happening, Meeta needed to be a part of it.

Also she was very smart; always an 'A' Grader and she could have had any career she chose, if only she had stuck to things she wanted to do and not get distracted with sacrificing every time for her family.

One thing about Meeta during college was that she made people around her comfortable, <u>except for me</u>, which is probably the reason for her popularity in college especially amongst the boys.

Unfortunately, me being an introvert and unable to speak to girls that well, the only sentence I could muster up in the 5 years of college was "Hi, I Am Anup, Can I be friends with you", to which Meeta's reply was even crisper "No". The only semblance of friendship, which I could garner with Meeta was because of Rakhi (Sunil and my sister) and Pooja who managed to join Meeta and her gang of friends during FY B.Com and through them, I managed to get a chance to at least float around her, but unable to speak to her.

Rakhi and I were close, since School and being my sister as well we continued to remain close.

Pooja was the only other girl I spoke to freely in college and she became our friend due to Aditya as she and Aditya were class mates. Pooja's house was like our evening joint where I and Udit used to go across to just sit down and chat. Pooja's mother and father were very fond of both me and Udit, towards me I can be sure because I was the only one allowed to drive their car. Pooja is now married to Udit's elder brother Umang and they have two lovely daughters.

In Meeta's group of girlfriends there were also many characters. There was Kuntal the purple girl with a purple fiat, purple pen, always dressed in purple pants with tom boyish swag. There was Rinku, the always chatty one with a 24 x 7 capacity to speak. Then there was Kanchan, the quiet one and the biggest fan of Pete Sampras. Finally there was Chandani and Runa. All of them later became my friends as well, but being a shy guy my conversation with these girls also never went beyond a few paragraphs.

But I was never disappointed with my college life. Yes, I could not become friends with Meeta, but I had a lot of fun in college as did Meeta.

I continued my passion for football, and because of my love for Hindi Songs, and inspired by Sanjay Dutt in Saajan, I become a poet as well and by the time I completed college I had written a whole book of short poems. See, I have a hidden talent as well,

During college our financial position was not that good so my pocket money was a daily allowance equal to, To and Fro Bus Fare along with 20 Rupees for Food and Snacks and if there were matches, then the allowance increased to 50 for food and snacks and travel.

Depending on how much money I managed to save up, food during college time was either just Bun Maska or Tea or when I was rich enough it was Kheema Pav and Cold Drink at Gul.

To show off sometime it would also be a sandwich at Subhash or a shared Triple Schezwan Rice at Snow Point or a Medu Vada Sambar at Mani's.

The first month in First Year Junior College, I religiously attended classes till the day; one of my classmates Faisal came across to me enquiring whether I was Anup. On confirmation he said the college sports in-charge was looking out for me as I had taken my admission in sports quota and he wanted to meet me. It was from that day, that I became an OUTSTANDING student.

Give me a chance to be on the football field I would take it. Whether it was travelling at 5:00 am in the morning to reach the ground to playing with 12 stitches on my head, I have done it all. So impressive was my keeping in those days that I even got selected to play for a 2nd Division Football Team in the Western Region Football Zone and would regularly be invited for various small tournaments all over Mumbai.

But one thing was sure in my mind and that was I would not be making Football my career as except for Cricket there was no money in any other sports and it was not possible to earn enough to run a household by playing. This I am saying from personal experience as when I used to play 2nd Division, my stipend was 50 Rupees per game, while I used to spend close to 30 Rupees just to reach the ground. So like a lot of things once I finished College, I packed up my Keeping gloves and never wore them again. But before I packed up, I still needed to get famous for the last time.

I have said earlier my name appeared two times in papers, the first incident I have narrated earlier. The second incident came when I was in SY B.com. For this I would like to thank Meeta. It was the week of my birthday and as was the practice, a cake was cut in the college green room and my face was turned into a canvas.

Meeta for the first time shook hands with me on this day and wished me. That same afternoon, I had our Inter College match with one of the top college team of Mumbai. The opposite team had international exchange students from Nigeria and they were a very tough team, but what a match we had. Not only did we win that match, but won it on penalties and next day since it was an upset, details of our match along with special praise for me was there in the sports section of Times of India.

Like I said, throughout my college days, there were "0" conversations which I had with Meeta and the "0" conversation record continued even after. So you will think how Meeta came into my life, if we never spoke. For this I have to thank Rinku.

After our exams were over and just before results, it was agreed between all of us that we would meet one last time and Rinku took the initiative and invited all of us to her house in Lonavala. It was there we all friends met her parents for the first time. We reached her place in the morning and immediately proceeded for Tiger Falls. We were all enjoying our time in the waterfall when all of a sudden Meeta slipped and fell, luckily for her, I and Aditya were near the end and we managed to hold onto her.

After this scary incident we all returned to Rinku's house and after lunch, we all boys came back to Mumbai with the girls continuing on with their stay. Believe me when I say, I thought this was the last time I would be seeing Meeta.

After our results in which I passed with 56% (good enough for me considering minimum criteria for CA or CS was 50% plus), I joined Ravi Mama in his company as an intern in Worli. All was forgotten by now, when out of the blue I got a call on my office Landline.

Somehow Rinku had managed to get Ravi Mama's office number from my mother. On the phone Rinku just asks me, where I am and when I can meet her. I said I am in Worli and can meet her anytime and she said meet me at 5:00 pm at Podar. Since Worli was around 20 minutes bus ride to Matunga I said yes and met Rinku at 5:00 p.m.

The first thing which Rinku asked me is "Whether I am still interested in Meeta". I was totally taken aback. After collecting my thoughts, I said "Yes, sure I am". Immediately Rinku said "So is Meeta". I was totally shocked. I said I don't believe her and she said she shall make me speak to Meeta, if I don't believe her.

I said "make me speak to Meeta"! And right then, from the PCO booth, Rinku called up Meeta and gave the phone to me. I did not know what to say and the first words which came out of my mouth were "Is It True?" to which after a couple of second wait the answer was "Yes". We did not speak any other single word after that.

After keeping the phone down, I asked Rinku to arrange a meeting between me and Meeta, which she readily arranged and it was decided that since Meeta used to go for her classes in Ghatkopar, we shall meet at Bharat Café which was next to the station.

From Bharat Café we went to Nariman Point. Since neither of us had ever been on a date, we did not know what to do. You won't believe, we sat on the benches in Nariman Point in the peak afternoon with me showing Meeta my poems.

We were so scared, that we never touched each other throughout our first date. The only point we agreed upon after our first meeting was that, we shall take forward our relationship only if our parents agreed upon it.

Since the agreement was made, immediately on returning home I told my mother and sister about Meeta and our first meeting. This I had to do as my parents were leaving the next day to attend a wedding and would be away for a week.

The same night Mummy spoke to Daddy about Meeta and like I have said my father is modern and conservative at the same time, luckily for me he was in his modern mood that day and gave a single sentence reply to me "OK, we shall meet her once we are back".

Now since I had set the ball rolling, Meeta also confided in her parents after a couple of days. Her parents first gave her a dressing down but after a day agreed to meet me at least once. I met Meeta's parents at a restaurant in Mulund. Meeta's father kept asking me all sorts of questions while Meeta's mom kept looking at me. One thing about Meeta's mom is that Meeta is a carbon copy of her.

Finally after 30 minutes of grilling, her father asked me about my Kundli (Birth Chart), I said it would be with my parents and then he asked me for the date and time of birth. I knew my date of birth but did not know my exact time of birth. But still since I had heard my mother previously mention that I was born around 4, I said 4:00 pm.

Meeta's father immediately within a day or two took my details to their Panditji to see whether we were a match. The reply was a 'NO' from their Panditji and accordingly Meeta communicated to me. Around this time, my mother had also called me to enquire how I was doing and during the conversation, I casually asked her what my time of birth was and she said it was 5:15 pm.

Immediately on keeping the phone down with my Mom, I called Meeta up and informed her that I had given the wrong time of birth and my correct time of birth was 5:15 pm. Meeta's father again took the revised details to his Panditji and luckily for me and Meeta, Panditji said 'YES'.

By this time my parents had come back to Mumbai from the wedding. After discussion with Meeta's parents it was agreed that both the sets of parents would meet once to discuss and see if things can be taken forward.

Between the times I met with Meeta at Bharat Café and then with her Parents, Meeta and I did not meet even once. The only time we spoke was when Meeta went to Rinku's place.

Meeta's elder sister Manju, had just got engaged and was set to be married off the next year, so at the time of the meeting apart from Meeta's parents and siblings there was Sunil, Manju's would be husband, Meeta's fathers sisters and their husbands. From our side there were my Parents and my Badi Mummy.

After the initial greetings, once we sat down, my mother and Badi Mummy went across to Meeta and presented her with a gold necklace and made her wear it as well. Meeta's mother was not there in the room at that time as she had gone to the Kitchen to arrange for snacks.

After meeting my Mummy and Badi Mummy, when Meeta went back to the Kitchen to help her mother, her mother seeing the necklace around Meeta, scolded her saying what has she done? Accepting the set meant the proposal has been accepted and now it cannot be undone, Lucky for me.

The very next week a small ceremony was conducted at Meeta's place and on 14th September the news of our relationship was announced to the world.

Waiting for Meeta to say Yes from 1991 to 1996 and then seeing things unfolding from the time I met Meeta at Bharat Café on 19th August 1996 to getting engaged with her on 14th September 1996, everything seem so unreal.

A question which remains unanswered is what happened between the time of our Lonavala trip and 18th August when Rinku met me in Matunga, but let's keep this story my little secret.

Here we were, me all of 20 years 11 months 22 days and Meeta all of 20 years 11 months 11 Days, engaged to be married.

After getting engaged to Meeta, you would be thinking as I did, that my life was done. What more would I have asked for.

I was getting married to the love of my life, my father had a decent income coming in from the hospital in which I was also working part time and I was on my way to completing my CS as well.

But I was wrong, way wrong. I was the Balraj Sahani from the film "Waqt", is how wrong I was. My actual challenges were just around the corner. My belief system got me Meeta, but making my life with Meeta tested my belief system to the core.

For every belief system to function, it needs oxygen, and the oxygen comes from that one person, whom he/she can rely on 100%, for me that one person was Meeta. I am sure you to will have your one special person.

Similarly for every belief system to keep growing it needs challenges and these challenges life keeps throwing at you all your lives, as it did mine. Whether it is the challenge pertaining to how you as a couple shall adjust to each other and your respective families, whether it is a challenge related to how you shall adjust to your workplace and grow, whether it is the challenges you face from your kids and how you shall nurture them, whether it is the challenge of adjusting to the society you live in. Man so many Challenges life keeps throwing at you.

In Meeta and my case, the first set of challenges pertained to Meeta adjusting to my family.

My family I have already introduced you to, so let me introduce Meeta's family to you as well.

Meeta has two more siblings, an elder sister Manju and a

younger brother Rajesh. Manju being the eldest was the rebel. She was and still is a very outspoken person. You cannot push Manju and expect to get away with it. Meeta, although outspoken and fun loving being the middle child, she was also very accommodative. Rajesh was the youngest but the most pampered.

Meeta's Father and Meeta's Grandmother ensured Rajesh remained the most pampered child.

Meeta's father like Meeta is a social animal; he cannot sit at home for more than a couple of hours. He had worked hard all his life and managed to make a name for himself in the Mulund Colony area. If there was a social event, Meeta's father would be there. It is probably from her father; Meeta got her genes for fun. Once Meeta's father returned back from work, the party in the house would start. Every second day was a movie, a dinner or an ice-cream party for the kids.

Meeta's Mom on the other hand was the homemaker. She was the only sister to 5 elder brothers who doted on her and do so even today. One habit of Meeta's Mom which probably Meeta has inculcated subconsciously is the habit of shouting out load.

The first thing I noticed about Meeta's Mom was her habit to shout out the names of her kids and the loud tone in which she used to speak to them. Meeta does the same with our kids as well now. In our house the two words you will hear most repeating are Shreesh and Prithvi. Meeta's Mom has a strong personality as she too has gone through a lot in her life and this is another trait of Meeta's Mom that Meeta has inculcated in her.

I have not introduced you to my brother in law Sunil. Sunil is another gem of a person, very family oriented and one of the calmest men I have met. He has his peculiar tastes as well, like the way he eats his food and what he eats. For him beer is a thing which should be there on all holidays, celebrations and vacations.

When we travel together, the best thing Sunil enjoys is just doing nothing; this is probably because of the hectic life he leads in Mumbai. But every Sunday he and his entire family make time by helping their Guru ji to run a charitable homeopathic clinic.

Another habit of Meeta that is being accommodative has continued till date and comes from her strong desire to balance things. Being a typical Libran, if Meeta sleeps till late one day, she has to get up early the next, if Meeta has gone with her friends one day and spent some personal time, immediately she would want to spend a day with me alone to balance it out. It is like a see-saw with her all the time, always sailing in two boats.

Meeta too is a family person from within and loves her family dearly. Like I can do anything for my family so can she. The only difference between me and Meeta probably is that she is just too sensitive by nature and just cannot hurt anyone and sometimes this leads to emotionally draining situations which she find's herself in. Probably, she and her family were also inspired by Ramanand Sagar ji and B R Chopra ji.

Initially the environment in my house in Chembur and Vashi was similar to the environment in Meeta's house. But unfortunately Meeta entered my life when I was staying in the hospital.

My house at the time I was getting married looked like a military house, with everything driven by the clock, breakfast by 10:00, Lunch by 2:00, Tea at 5:00 and Dinner at 9:00 with TV remote in Daddy's hand and we all kids either sitting erect in front of him or sitting in our rooms. Meeta's house on the other hand resembled a fun and fair zone, with songs being sung, games being played, eating food at odd hours and very little of TV watching.

My father is a very loving person, but his experience of being alone separated from his siblings has made him develop a shell around himself. This shell does not easily allow people to come close to him, probably because he does not want to feel hurt again. But this shell managed to keep Meeta out for a very long time and even me getting into that shell is never easy.

The only time the shell is removed is when my father is with his siblings or when he is organizing a party. At these occasions a completely different personality of my father comes forth and then the fun side of my father takes over. The mutton and the barbeque which my father makes are legendary and the parties which we used to have when we are all together, I am sure none of us will ever forget in our lives. Even my friends say that the best mutton they have eaten is at my place cooked by my Dad. My father in fact has had drinks with all my friends in front of me and he quite likes sitting with them whenever they come over.

The problems between my Daddy and Meeta, originated because of my desire to spend maximum time with Meeta during my courtship period which lasted 18 months. My Dad became insecure because he felt; Meeta would pull me away from him as what had happened with his other siblings. But hopefully now after 22 years of staying together, my Daddy does not have the same set of insecurities towards Meeta. But still he misses his siblings a lot and his shell is still there.

Over the next 18 months of courtship, Meeta got a good taste of what she was getting into and believe me she was shit scared. The incidence of selecting Meeta's bridal dress was one such incidence which showed how scared she was.

As was the tradition, the Bridal dress is given by the Grooms family and Meeta had come with me, my mother and father to select the same. Normally girls like to do some window shopping, trying different stuff before picking their final choice. Nothing of this sort was allowed with my Daddy around.

My father took us to the biggest shop in Dadar, picked out the most expensive Saree which was of Red Colour and gave to Meeta to try on. Meeta hated it but since she was scared all she could say was "Yes, Daddy Very Nice, Let's Buy It".

So scared was Meeta, that if anyone had come up to her at that time just before marriage and told her it was ok to walk away from this marriage, she would have done so. Not because of me (she had fallen by now deeply in love with me), but because of how scared she was of facing my father. Luckily for me no one did.

After a few of months of my engagement and after giving a couple of CS Inter Exams and not managing to clear them, I decided to quit the CS program and decided that I would now work full time in the hospital and manage the affairs of the hospital and that would be my source of livelihood.

Meeta's and my wedding was a huge affair. Probably influenced by his own wedding, my Daddy wanted to have a similar wedding for his son. He invited all his siblings and relatives and except for Raj Didi who could not make it due to visa issues as she was living abroad, all made it.

The wedding was a full 10 day affair and the entire Hospital was converted to a party zone, with guests staying in the hospital and dance parties every evening.

Drinks were stocked in all fridges and what my friends Sunil and Purvesh remember the most about my wedding is the amount of beer they had. "Hum Aapke Hain Kaun" inspired our family as well and to show we are a single unit, we decided to wear similar clothes for the wedding functions as well. Our Band Bajha look was memorable.

Here we were, I all of 23 years 4 months 9 days and Meeta 23 years 3 months 29 days starting our life together.

The icing on the distance cake between my Daddy and Meeta was thanks to Shweta and her love for me. Like a loving sister, on the night of my wedding, she decided to celebrate the occasion with a bottle of champagne which would be opened by her in our wedding suite along with all of our friends.

After the reception which ended at around 2:00 am, by the time we reached the hotel room, it was 3:00 am. As soon as we entered there was Shweta and our group of friends ready with a nice bottle of champagne.

We would have just opened the bottle of champagne when in walked my Daddy. 6-7 pegs down and at the height of his conservative mood and here was Meeta, with a big smile of her face and a glass of champagne in her hand. One look from Daddy and the party was over not only that day but for quite a long time for Meeta as my father could not take out his anger on me or Shweta. Luckily things did improve, and now Daddy actually likes Meeta to a large extent.

The relationship which Meeta shares with my mother is that of a typical Mother in Law, Daughter in Law one. Hot and cold, if one was hot the other was cold and if the other got hot, then the other would become cold. But it was fun and is still fun the way they continue to have their daily discussion.

The best relationship which Meeta shared in the house was with Badi Mummy. She supported Meeta the most. It all started when Meeta as per the tradition in our house was supposed to cook her first meal for the family. Meeta being Meeta had never entered the Kitchen before she got engaged to me and her cooking skills were under developed during our courtship period. So now when the time came to cook in my house, Meeta would have started crying if it was not for Badi Mummy.

Badi Mummy realized Meeta could not cook and stepped in and told Meeta, she shall do the cooking part and Meeta can just help give the final touches and serve the food. Since Badi Mummy had said this, no one could question the decision and Meeta was saved. From that day onwards Badi Mummy was Meeta's favourite. I also think Badi Mummy reminded Meeta of her Nani and hence she loved her a lot.

The others in the family easily welcomed Meeta and for my cousins she was their Bhabhi, their first Bhabhi as well as friend.

Here was Meeta, coming from a fun loving environment where any one could say anything to one another; to a family which to Meeta resembled as if they were living in a concentration camp, all strict and proper, was brain shattering for her.

The combination of my father's strictness, my mother's strong nature and Meeta's brain shattering experiences in my house and her overtly sensitive nature, got me into a self-realization zone. I realized that by now all elements of a bomb have been stacked up properly in my house and the action of anyone in the house had the potential to explode it.

I am sure everyone who has married has gone through this self-realization.

Another thing which bothered Meeta the most after marriage was the fact that her parents had taken sizeable loans to marry the two daughters. Manju had got married on 30th December 1996 while Meeta got married on 1st February 1998. Manju's wedding like my wedding was also an elaborate affair. Both these marriages along with the new house which my father in law had constructed had drained the family of all their savings and Meeta being Meeta was most affected by it.

So the challenge became more complicated with more ingredients now added.

So now you will ask, how did I and Meeta manage these challenges? Don't worry this million dollar answer of how you can manage these challenges which is there in everyone's house, I shall provide to you soon, so please read on.

 Not everything in Meeta and my life was serious, we did also have a lot of fun together and the fun started on our honeymoon.

For our honeymoon, I had booked a one way train ticket to Jammu and had taken 50,000 from Daddy with a plan to come back once that money was exhausted. Meeta and I had no clue where we would go and had decided we shall decide on the way.

Ensuring that we are able to extend the trip to the max level possible was our only goal, and this required planning and luckily for us, we met two great couples, Viral and Sunita who like us had a love marriage and Sanjay and Jyoti who had a traditional arranged one. Even they were on a budget as us and it was decided that to conserve cash it would be better we share our transport and try and get the best deals in the hotels as negotiating for 3 rooms would be better than one.

What a sight we were, three couples in one Ambassador with a crazy driver. You should have seen him drive, probably was a truck driver and the Ambassador was a toy compared to the one he must have driven previously.

Our best ride was the one we had from Dalhousie to Khajiar. The road had just been cleaned of the snow and there was literally 5-6 foot high snow wall on both side of road, what a sight it was.

Viral, Sunita and we were more interested in sight-seeing while Sanjay and Jyoti were more interested in checking out the room. Our rooms were cold most of the time with all four of us shivering while here was Sanjay and Jyoti with a permanent heater on in their room sitting way too comfortable for us.

We travelled all over north, from Jammu we went to Vaishno Devi, did our darshans and then we went to Patni Top and from there to Dharmashala and from there to Dalhousie and from there to Manali and finally to Delhi and then back to Mumbai all this under 50,000.

I and Meeta also had our first tiff on our honeymoon at Dharmashala but luckily for me, the tiff ended very fast and we had a nice Candle Light dinner.

Sanjay and Jyoti did not join us on the Manali leg and they returned back to Mumbai from Dalhousie. Viral and Sunita continued on with us to Manali and then to Delhi. Sanjay and Jyoti did not meet us after that trip, but Sunita and Viral are still in touch.

Sunita, Viral and we have had many such wonderful trips over the last 22 years we have known each other. Like us Sunita and Viral have two children, one daughter and a son.

The words which best describe this phase is,

'Love is a mystery never to be understood,

But to be felt,

Love can make you do crazy things and

Those of who, who have fallen in love

Have felt it first-hand,

In your love life,

Your feeling keeps going up and down

And it is these ups and downs

Which make Life Worth Living'

My Belief System also picked up a few pointers from Meeta and my experiences and they were,

- Never lose hope as things shall always get better and if things have to happen they shall happen

- Once Committed, there can be just no one else and no going back on what you have been committed to

- If people don't accept you as a person that does not mean you need to change just for that person to accept you, but you can always keep working on improving yourself

Chapter 8 - My Juniors, Colleagues and Seniors

In today's world a person, spends more time at his work place than in his personal space interacting with his family. Since you are spending at least 1/3rd of your time at work, it is important that you are in the right frame of mind when there. To be in the right frame of mind you need to be comfortable at your work place.

Before you join your work place, you have already lived a life for around 20-25 years and already developed a belief system which is the foundations of your core, so being comfortable at a work place for me, means a place where one is not changing his belief system just to fit in.

Since Life for me meant moving ahead, I experienced a variety of things in my career.

- From being a small boy managing part time a small hospital in Navi Mumbai

- To becoming a data entry operator in a Publishing Company

- To then becoming an Accountant in that same Publishing Company

- To becoming a Junior Executive in an IT Company

- To moving to Saudi Arabia in a Telecom Company

- To becoming a Manager in a Telecom Company

- To becoming a CFO of a Division

- To moving to Sales

- To becoming a Regional Head

- To giving up everything and coming back to begin the journey all over again

During this entire journey, I met a lot of people, who along the way helped me grow and become a better person. I call them my influencers as well.

My first sets of influencers were the Doctors, Chemists, Pharma and Medical Equipment executives whom I interacted with during the days I was managing the hospital. From all of them I learnt for the first time not everyone is equal and everyone has different set of priorities in their life and the medical fraternity is not what I thought it was.

I also got to know the system of cuts and how that works and I did not like what I saw and hence *the only lesson I learnt from this experience was it is better to move out of a work place if things make you do things which are against your core* and this experience was going against the learning I got from Ramanand Sagar ji and B R Chopra Ji also and so I moved out. Just Kidding…

I moved out because I was having a lot of free time at hand and there was no expansion plans in the offerings at the hospital and it was best for me that I move out of my family hospital set up and try and make my career somewhere else and that is what exactly I did.

Before I get into my professional life, I would like to make a disclaimer here. I am using abbreviations / initials of companies and people who have influenced me to ensure that the narration does not get digressed into personalities and the main reason of writing these memoirs is not lost.

The second set of lesson I learnt in my professional life was from RJV Sir the CFO of JL. During my stint in the publishing house, although the vacancy required a CA, RJV Sir selected me for the Accountants position as he thought I had the required skill set needed. To give you a small glimpse of my life in JL read on.

The atmosphere in JL being a Media house was filled with banter, there was the editorial team always discussing ideas for the next issue, the designing team working on the visualization part, the marketing team working on ensuring advertisers were on board.

The regular fights between the marketing and editorial teams on paid articles and how they should be incorporated into the issue, the designing team and their monthly fights with the editorial team as they needed to give the final product to the printers on a particular date and time. It was total chaos but believe me every month all the issues still came out on time. It was like everything used to come into place just before the deadline.

Being part of the accounts team, our work was smooth sailing for 20 days in the month when the pressure was on the editorial, marketing and designing team, but during the last 10 days of the month, we were to sweat it out.

Getting the bills generated, getting the pay roll processed, completing the accounting for all sales and expenses by 30th of every month to ensure that on 1st of the next month, the final monthly accounts, magazine wise are made available with the Management.

The deadline aspect of reports by 1st or 2nd of the month was paramount because there was a monthly printing cycle, correction if any on any aspect of the business if required to be made needed to be made prior to the work on the next issue starting, as changing anything mid-month was not possible.

In JL we had an open environment where you were heard at least at the senior management level if not the ownership level even if you were a Junior Executive.

These strict guidelines from RJV Sir and the environment in JL taught me my most important business lessons which were,

- *Say what you have to say, always*

- *Decisions have to be taken*

- *But Decisions need to be taken based on data*

- *And Timing is the most important thing in decision making*

I moved from JL because my life was stagnating and the work there was becoming a routine. Since my belief system relied on 'Moving Ahead', I had to move and I moved.

In my next stint in GS and GL, I used these learning from JL very effectively and this led me to my initial success in GS.

But my time in GS and GL was also one learning phase after another.

To make you understand what these learnings were, I will have to tell you the story of my experiences in GS and GL in more detail as I spent the next 19 years of my life in these organizations.

I was introduced to GS by my friend Udit, who had moved from JL to GS and he informed me about an opening in his organization. GS was in the Information and Technology space and I did know anything about IT. My computer knowledge was limited to connecting the desktop, powering it on and letting the system do the booting as it normally does and start using the software's which are there on the desktop.

Since, I did not know anything about IT before I went for the interview; I went through the website of my future company. I could not make held or tail of what this company did as this company was into set up of Virtual Private Networks, Data Centre and Deployment and Management of Office Networking Equipment and for me all this was alien. But I went across confidently as the maximum which could go wrong would be that I would be thrown out of the interview but since I had never been interviewed before at least I shall get this experience as well.

My interview experience though was a very funny one. The vacancy for which I was being interviewed was that of a Junior Executive – Budgets. I had heard of Accounts as a stream but what was this Budget about, so I asked EV, who was the HR Manager and responsible for filling up this vacancy.

He answered that this vacancy is because there is a gap between Projects and Accounts and the project team does not want to spend their time feeding data to Accounts and the Accounts team does not have the time explaining the financial constraints to the projects team. To solve this problem, a person from accounts background will get involved with the project team and that is why the opening.

The description was essentially that of a postman between E2 where Project Team sat and E1 were the Accounts Team sat. E2 and E1 are two building in Navi Mumbai, next to each other.

After meeting EV, my first level interview was with YS, who was the DGM Accounts and was reporting to SN Sir who was the CFO. My interview with YS went off well, with YS asking me some basic questions which luckily I could answer. After meeting YS in E1, I was asked to go across and meet the project head KK Sir in E2.

KK Sir was a very senior person and everyone in the company was shit scared of him. Luckily for me, probably I got him in his good mood and I had a good chat with him. He did not ask me anything about accounts, but about my background and what I had done previously. Probably KK Sir liked my frankness when I told him clearly that I have no experience of the business in which the company was involved in but would like to learn about it.

After this meeting with KK Sir, I was supposed to meet SN Sir. While I was walking back from E2 to E1, I thought to myself, what would I do if I got the job, should I move from JL where

I was happy and comfortable to this new set up where I did not know anything.

I again said to myself, what the hell, if they select me let me take the jump and see if I can swim in this company as well. By the time I walked from E2 to E1 and had done my introspection, KK Sir had called up SN Sir and told him, he like me. The first words of SN Sir, I still remember "Oh you, you are selected as KK has selected you". The way he said sounded more like he was relieved than anything else.

Such was the desperation for filling this vacancy up that, the negotiations for pay package happened there and there itself. EV asked me how much I wanted as salary. I said give me more than I am getting now and I shall be Ok. I informed him that I was getting 7800 approx. and immediately I got an offer letter from EV with my pay being increased to 10,000. Between 11:00 am and 4:00 pm, everything was done including lunch which EV was kind enough to arrange for me.

I had not informed or consulted anyone back home about it, but since I had already committed to it, I went ahead with putting in my papers in JL and moving to GS.

I joined GS on 5th June 2000. After completing my joining formalities, I was told to sit in E2. My designation was Executive – Budgets, which was a step lower than the level I had at JL, where I was a Senior Executive – Accounts. But like I have said, I have a habit of moving on and not looking back.

I did not look back in spite of the fact that my pay scale also decreased when I joined GS, from taking a net pay salary of

7,818 to now getting 7,218 as GS had a very different pay roll processing system than JL and it is in GS that I understood the concept of CTC (Cost to Company). But like I said, once I move on, I move on.

A work station was allocated to me and after basic rounds of introduction I was told I would be informed what I would need to do later. I was given a bunch of literature to read and that was all. For one whole month, I did nothing but read the literature given and waited to be told what to do.

Since the rest of my colleagues in E2 were technical project guys, I did not know what to chat with them, so I used to go across to E1 to have my lunches as Udit used to sit in E1. Because of Udit's friendly and jovial nature, he had settled nicely in GS and through him I got to know the entire ERP implementation team and the entire Accounts Team.

Since, I was not used to sitting idle and since my reason for coming to GS was to learn, after a month I went up to KK Sir and asked him what he wanted me to do. He point blank told me to talk to SN Sir as I was supposed to fulfil SN Sir and Accounts team requirements of data gathering from Project Team.

Now, I understood the meaning of duel reporting. Although I am working in Projects, my KRA was to be finalized by Accounts.

- *My first lesson learnt was, what DUEL REPORTING is all about. If you don't know what to do with a resource that needs to work in two departments, use the Duel*

Reporting system to mess him up and ensure the two department heads he has to interact with have their Egos protected.

So I went to SN Sir, SN Sir in his own style told me to talk to YS as it is YS who needs Data from projects to consolidate in books. YS like his name asked me why I have come to him. To which when I replied that SN Sir has sent me, he said wait let me talk to SN Sir. I waited and when he came back, he told me he shall give me some work to be done later.

I waited for a whole week and after a week I got a bunch of Telephone bills on my desk. I was told I needed to check them and approve their payments from the projects team.

Here, I was with a whole bunch of Telephone bills and totally clueless as what I am supposed to do. Luckily for me, by now in project team I had made a couple of friends and I went up to them and asked them some basic questions.

- First – Where are all these telephone lines?

- Second – What do we do with these telephone lines?

- And Third – Do we need so many telephone lines?

I got the answers to the first two questions but for the third there was no answer. For the 3rd question, the answer I got was these lines were requested at the time the initial deployment was happening and no one has reviewed it as there was no process of review or checking and no one even knew that these needed to be checked.

After studying three to four past bill cycles, I gave a report to KK Sir and SN Sir identifying the gaps in their system. I identified 1000 odd lines which we were paying for but these lines were not terminated in any of our offices.

Similarly, I found out that although we had close to 8000 lines terminated all across India, we actually needed only around 6,000 based on our current subscriber base. This report gained me some level of respect and I became the Telephone Line Guy.

Since, I was attached to the projects, the approval of all project and marketing team expense voucher was the next assignment I got.

A simple exercise of Voucher checking was also a task in GS at that time, as again no one had the time to check the fine print. Since GS was part of a big listed company there were policies for everything and anything. There was a lot of fine print to read in every policy. Limits were set, but exceptions also mentioned in the fine print. It was as if an English Lawyer had written these policies on the lines of how they would have written a law. For every rule there was a sub rule which overruled the main rule.

Lucky for me I had tried my luck at being a Company Secretary and as part of my study material was reading up laws laid down towards company operations and understanding the fine print. The first thing I did before I started checking vouchers was read the policies along with the fine print.

Because I had read the fine print, I could advice people effectively and soon I became the voucher man apart from being the lines man. These are not my words, they are the words with which I was awarded at the GS Annual conference which had taken place in Goa in 2001.

I was actually given the award for the best Junior Executive in the Support Functions for effectively checking vouchers and bills, crazy yeah.

Again from a 'Nobody', I become a 'Somebody'.

- *My Second lesson learnt was, in Big Companies simple things also become a task requiring resources and planning and execution because discussions are replaced by what is written in the process and policies and what is written in the process and policies is too complicated at times for any sane person to understand.*

In GS, the finance function was split into 2 parts, Accounts and Treasury. SN Sir handled the Accounts Function while CVK Sir handled the Treasury Function. In my second year at GS, the merger with GL happened and with this there was re-alignment of roles. CVK Sir became my boss with SN Sir moving to the Call Centre Business.

With CVK Sir, everything was about a one pager. Any proposal which had to be taken to CVK Sir had to be accompanied by a one pager summary that had all major points or highlights of the proposal. Since all proposals were from Projects and I was the designated Project Guy, it was my duty to summarize all proposals into a one pager and present it to CVK Sir.

To do this, I had to develop in-depth knowledge of everything that went on in Projects and I did. Whether it was Bandwidth sizing to

Date Centre Rack pricing, I learnt about everything. The concept of the Dashboard was getting developed in me, Since, I was also good with Contracts, reviewing of them also came to me.

- _My Third lesson learnt in GL was essentially what I had learnt in JL from RJV Sir that understanding how your business works is very important as without knowing what your business is and what you do in your business and how you make money, you cannot be an effective accountant or commercial person._

The purpose of joining this company which was to learn was being achieved.

After the merger with GL went through in 2001-2002, GS become the ES within GL. Along with ES there were two other business streams, CC and NE.

Within a week of Meeta expressing her desire to experience life at least for some time away from my parents, I got a call from CVK Sir, telling me whether I would be interested in going to Saudi Arabia for a short period of time.

On enquiring as to what I needed to do in Saudi Arabia, I was told NE Division was setting up business operations in Saudi Arabia and they had won a big order there and if I was selected I would be the Deputy General Manager reporting to the Country CFO. As was my habit, giving me something new to learn along with a possibility of fulfilling Meeta's wish was an exciting combination and hence I accepted the challenge, in spite of the location being Saudi Arabia.

The selection process however took 3 months. Finally, I was selected, probably for two reasons, reason one I did not negotiate on my Salary, reason two I again admitted that I have no knowledge of NE business but that I would learn.

The only condition I laid from my side was that I would go on a family visa and company would have to take care of my family's visa and tickets to Saudi Arabia, which they agreed to.

Since, I raised the point of going with my Family the management probably thought I was their best bet as if I went with my family chances of me coming back fast would be reduced.

My selection finally came through in the month of June 2002 and I was supposed to fly to Saudi Arabia on 30th of July 2002.

Once the selection was through, I was told I would be trained on NE Business and be informed exactly what I was supposed to do in Saudi Arabia. As learning anything new, excites me, I joined my new team. In those days, NE division was located in E1 and so I moved from E2 to E1.

The first person I met there was MN Sir (Captain as he is called), who was the CFO and also one of the person in my interview panel. Captain gave me some contracts to read and told me that my job was the most important and critical job in the entire company. I am supposed to raise all invoices to the customers, track all collections and payments.

Since invoicing was the most important job, I was told to sit with AG who used to sit just outside Captains office and learn how to do invoicing. I sat with AG for 15 minutes and understood it. Then I was told to sit with RM and SS who used to do payment checking.

Again sat with them for an hour and was done. Finally I was introduced to SD, PP, PJ and TN, who were the people who used to interact with the project team and were responsible for the contract management part. It was thanks to all four of them that I got a chance to go to Saudi as initially they were the original choices and it was only when they declined to go to Saudi that I got a chance to go. SD later went to Sri Lanka with TN moving to Bangladesh and then to UK and PJ later went to Saudi.

I landed up in Riyadh, Saudi Arabia on 30th July 2002 along with DT who was supposed to handle the Administration Department. DT was an old trusted lieutenant in GL.

The first thing DT told me at the Airport when we met was, take off your gold chain and gold rings. I asked him why and he said, if I don't take it off, I would be questioned by Saudi immigrations as wearing Gold by men is haram in Islam.

During the entire flight I was made aware of my dos and don'ts in Saudi Arabia. So by the time I landed in Saudi I started thinking whether I had done the right thing or not by taking up this assignment. Before immigration I removed my rings and buttoned up my shirt so that my chain could not be seen. Immigration went off smoothly and after collecting my luggage came Customs time.

In Saudi there are two lines for customs, one for ladies, families and white people and the other for bachelors coming from Pakistan, India, Bangladesh and such third world countries.

Since, I was alone and from India, although I had a white skin, I was made to stand in the third world line.

Before me I could see how the Saudi Immigration where checking the luggage. Food articles are thrown off in the dustbin, anything resembling religious texts or symbols of other religions were thrown as well, essentially the entire bags were turned upside down.

The family line and White Skin People line had an X-Ray machine to scan the bags and their bags were never opened.

Luckily for me I was not carrying any of this stuff and went through smoothly.

Outside the airport was another character who was waiting for me and DT, he was VK. VK was a relative of the MD of our company. He had reached Saudi a couple of months back and was DT's Junior Executive in Admin. His job was to receive all people at the airport and do whatever odd assignments were required to be done and instruct all those coming as to what are the Do's and Don'ts in Saudi Arabia.

After picking us up, we were dropped at Al Diyafa Apartments and Suites, which was a Hotel in Olaya District which lets out 1 BHK Apartments. Our company had taken on yearly lease a dozen apartments where all the Senior Engineers, Project Managers and Support staff were put up. We were 3 in One Apartment, me, DT and OP our HR Head.

Next day before starting for our office, OP informed me and DT that wearing a Tie in office by all Support Staff was mandatory.

Since we had not got any ties, OP lent us his. It was like a culture in Saudi, all expats wear Tie and Suits to office while local Saudi wear their traditional attire.

On our first day in office, I and DT were introduced to everyone in the office. Since everyone knew DT, it was only me who got formally introduced. Our office lay out was a strange one. On entering the office, there were cabins lined up around the edges, like a "D" with a large open space in the middle.

I was made to sit in a cabin which had two desks. One was given to PJ who was the Internal Auditor and second was given to me.

Our Corporate team in those days when I landed up there comprised of JS who was the Country Head, AT who was the CFO and my boss, CS who handled Sales, OP who was HR Manager, Ayman (an Egyptian) who was our Accountant, Javed who was Junior Executive Accounts, DT who started handling Admin and Kalam who was the office boy.

OP as the HR Manager had laid down certain practices in the office like wearing a Tie, morning and afternoon tea would be served in the conference room only were all people will assemble. This was a good thing and these meetings helped me settle as well and I encouraged such meetings in my team as well when I got a chance.

After a few months JS left for US and AT Sir took over the additional responsibilities of Country Head and we were also joined by another Sales Head to head the Function. NE's

Middle East Operations was controlled from Dubai with JR heading the same.

JR Sir, Anna as he was popularly called, was an old stalwart of GL as well. His connect and friend circle in Middle East was simply great. He was a total people's person, always joking around having fun. He was and still is a very avid cricketer.

Apart from our corporate office in Al Akaria Commercial Centre in Olaya, were we used to sit, we also had a project office which was essentially a Villa in which ground floor was used as project office and on first floor junior engineers and technicians used to stay.

I was taken to the project office the next day for introductions. There I met AV Sir who was heading the Project Team, MK, NM and AD who were the project managers. There were other project engineers like Anil, Shiva, Moin, Vikas, Vishwas and Arun and others whom I was also introduced to. VK the guy who picked us up from the airport was stationed here to look after the needs of the project team.

I was also introduced to AMZ Group CFO who was an Egyptian. Any company which wants to do business in Saudi Arabia needs to have a local sponsor and in our case it was AMZ. AMZ was a company owned by a Prince of Saudi Arabia and owing to their influence, we were able to get entry into Saudi Telecom Company and get ourselves impanelled with them.

In Al Diyafa evenings were a party, especially Thursday evenings. Friday all shops and restaurants in entire Saudi Arabia were closed till 3:00 pm in the afternoon and would open only after the afternoon prayers were over. With nowhere to go and eat, we used to try our best to be awake till very late on Thursday night, either sitting in the lobby of Al Diyafa or in someone's room, playing cards or just sitting around drinking Non Alcoholic Beer, just to ensure we got up late on Friday and skip lunch.

By the time I reached Riyadh, OP had made his arrangements and we followed it. Afternoon Lunch was a tiffin service which used to be delivered to our office and evening Dinner was at Manickal a small restaurant in Sulimaniyah. Our corporate office worked 5 days a week while the project office had a 6 day week.

Corporate office 5 day week was because the commercial centre in which our office was located was closed on Thursday and Fridays. If we had to work on Thursday we needed to register with the security personal in the centre to ensure that if there is a theft, the security personal had details of all people who were in the commercial centre for questioning. So we avoided working on Thursdays and Fridays.

The first two week went off well as there was nothing much to do. The project with Saudi Telecom Company (STC) was just starting so there was very little load.

However, the second week started off on a bad note. One of our Project Managers NM met with a car accident and expired. The entire atmosphere in the office changed. PJ who was staying in the same room with the NM, started having nightmares and it was decided that he shall move into our room for the time being, OP and DT in the room and me and PJ in the hall.

After a week or so, another incident happened in which my boss AT Sir came to my rescue. I had gone to the project office as instructed by AT Sir to collect the Purchase Orders issued by Project Team along with details of other expenses incurred. Probably I rubbed off AV Sir wrongly as he misunderstood my request for these details as interference in his work.

Probably, he was also disturbed with the death of his colleague and out came the anger on me. I was literally thrown out of the Project Office with the words, that if AT Sir wants to see or collect the documents, then he needs to come to Project Office and not send his deputies.

After being thrown out I thought it would be better I return back to India as my job was interacting with the project team and if the project head itself does not want me to interact with him then it would be better I return back.

Another reason subconsciously why probably I wanted to return back were the stories told to me by DT when he was travelling with me to Riyadh and the story told to me by OP when OP, HD Sir (Go to Man in NE), MK and AV Sir were hit by Eggs by a group of Saudi youngsters, while returning back from JS Sir's house after dinner. I was told this was a routine affair with Saudi Youngsters targeting expats for fun on weekends, so late night outings were ruled out from that day going forward.

Luckily for me, AT Sir remained calm and spoke to AV Sir and defused the situation and I also thought I needed to be braver if I were to succeed in life, so I stayed back. After a couple of days, I again went to the project office and this time AV Sir was kind enough to cooperate with me.

- *<u>My Fourth lesson learnt in GL was seeing the behaviour of AT Sir and how calmly he handled the situation with AV Sir. There was no compromise on what needed to be done but the things were managed by showing respect to each other.</u>*

From that day onwards I did not have any problem with any of my project team guys. In fact we became real good friends in the subsequent years. AV Sir being too senior was never a friend but he did guide me well and later I joined his NL Team when I returned to India. A big thanks to AT Sir for the way he handled the situation which allowed me to stay in Saudi and gave me the confidence that I have a boss who shall back me.

Like I had said, I was new to the NE business stream and the only experience I had was the few days I had spent with Captain and his team in India. Here another person came forward to help me out in understanding what NE was all about and that was PJ, who was the internal auditor.

PJ has a habit of eating Gutka or Pan Masala, but in spite of it being banned in Saudi he still managed to source this stuff and enjoyed it in Saudi Arabia as well. He was a Cost Accountant and had been with NE division for a couple of years now. Although from Orissa he had worked in Chennai and was well versed with Tamil language as well.

Since he had much more experience than me and since we were cabin partners, I started interacting with him to understand the business that NE did. I must appreciate here that PJ was kind enough to share his knowledge with me and I must say that whatever success I had in NE later, PJ was one of the reasons for it.

Normally, Accountants and Auditors have an estranged relationship as Auditors are supposed to audit the Accountants work and find out his mistakes, but PJ and I become good friends and remained so till I left GL. Why we are not in touch now is a different story for some other time.

The only instance me and PJ had a tiff was when in one of the reviews, a point was raised by PJ which implied something on me and my team's character. I immediately answered back stating if PJ had any proof on my mismanagement or that I or my team had made the company incur a loss, I would resign immediately from the company and leave the team.

Luckily for me, PJ understood my nature soon and never in my 19 years in GL, was any question raised on my integrity.

I coming from a family of businessmen and from my days in managing the hospital had realized one thing and that was, business was all about making hard cash. There was no concept of book money in my dictionary and it is because of this reason that I had my first tiff with the senior management of NE during my first year in Saudi.

My point of contention was a very simple point, I shall consider any revenue which the end customer certifies as completed and shall not take self-certification as the basis of recognizing revenue in the books. Although, my boss AT Sir was with me and understood why I had taken a particular stand, I did have issues with our Division President.

In one of our Annual Conferences, CN Sir even pulled me up from the entire crowd gathered and stated that here was Anup, who does not like to listen to his President as well on matters of how company figures are to be compiled and interpreted.

Thanks to the efforts of the Project Team who worked really hard combined with financial prudence, Saudi operations became a cash cow for NE Division. The issues with CN Sir soon resolved as he too understood that I had the best interest of the company in my mind.

- *My Fifth, Sixth and Seventh lesson learnt in GL which I also learned in JL was, It is essential to seek help to succeed as one is not expected to know everything and seeking help does not mean you are weak, similarly you need to know whom to seek help from as getting the knowledge from the right source is as important as seeking and finally when it comes to your integrity and self-beliefs don't take things lying down.*

    - *LEARNING = POSITIVITY (You Going Out To Seek Help and Not Being Told to Seek Help) + Self (Doing it because you are seeking for the knowledge) + People (Accepting that you don't have that Knowledge and you need to take this knowledge from people around you)*

The iqama which was a type of Work Permit are issued in two colours in Saudi, Green for Muslins and Brown for all other religions and once I received my Brown Iqama, I was able to get Meeta and Shreesh to Riyadh on 3rd December 2002.

Riyadh or for that matter Saudi Arabia is a strange place to live in. As long as you follow the guidelines of the kingdom, you are Ok and the guidelines are simple, if you are a Muslim pray 5 times and follow all the rules that a Muslim needs to follow and if you are a Non-Muslim male or female then do not disturb the Muslims when they are following their rituals and if you are a non-Muslim female you also need to wear the Abaya, cover your hair and if you're a Hindu Female you also need to wear the Bindi but you can show your face. The Bindi was the visa to show your face for a Hindu Female in Saudi Arabia.

There were areas where only Muslims could go and any person with a brown Iqama could not. If you are a bachelor you need to eat separately from where the families eat, if you are bachelor you also cannot enter parks and malls. You cannot look or stare at any female in public places and cannot disturb any female who is walking down the road.

To implement these rules, a type of Religious Police Force was there called the Mutawa's and they could have you arrested as well.

It is only now that Females have been allowed to drive but when I was there, no females were allowed to drive. Now I hear there are female call centre in Riyadh and shops which are exclusively managed by females for female customers, so there has been progress since the time I left.

Another thing which was very particular to Saudi was how the authorities behaved. If you are an expat your entire existence depends on your Sponsor. You can exit only when the sponsor allows you too.

If you have a car accident and you are an expat, the police shall come, take photographs of the incident, pick you up and place you in the police station. Only when your sponsor comes and releases you, can you then go home, till such time you can enjoy Kabsa Rice at the police station. Basic rules for an expat are if you do anything against the rules of the Kingdom then it is Jail then depending on your Sponsor's support a possibility of a Bail. Another speciality of Saudi was the blood principle.

If there is an accident and anyone dies, the person responsible for the accident has to settle with the family of the person who has died. Settlement is simple, blood for blood or money for blood.

If an expat died transfer of body back to his home, was one long process in Saudi. I had personal experience of how difficult it is to get a body transferred when one of our engineer died in a road accident and how I and CS ran from pillar to post to get the body transferred. In spite of our best efforts and contacts from as high as a Princes office, it took a good 20 days before we were able to send the body back.

The calls which CS and I used to receive from the parents of the person who had died were heart crushing. While we were doing this process, I came to know that there were at least 80-100 bodies of Indians who had died in Saudi whose bodies were lying in morgues all over Saudi Arabia for more than 6-8 months due to incompletion of paperwork.

For me, since my family was paramount and I was responsible for keeping them safe and considering the rules of the kingdom,

I was always on tenterhooks. If anything happened to me or if I was put in jail, I knew Meeta would have a horrible time getting me out. So in spite of my life being very nice in Saudi, I was not comfortable from within.

There was angst in me on two accounts. The first being I missed my family back home in India and second was that I had never felt like a second class citizen ever in my life, but in Saudi although everything was good, but the feeling of being a second class citizen always made me uncomfortable.

In India when I was growing up, since I had not personally experienced discrimination I thought we did not have it in India. But now when I actually experienced it, I realized that in India too we have been doing the same thing with others all our lives, in fact in my family itself we have been practicing such discrimination and I have also been practicing it all my life.

The classification of people on the lines that you are either with us or against us is also another form of discrimination. Now again I am feeling that same cringe inside of me after a long time, but this probably for a next time.

Money was good, life was good but this feeling of being a second class citizen made me cringe from inside and therefore once I completed my 2 year commitment which I had given to GL Management, I decided to return to India.

On the professional front, I did a lot of things for the first time like finalizing the books of accounts, getting the same Audited from professional auditors like Ernst and Young, filling all statutory returns, managing relationship with banks and AMZ and getting a strong understanding of what financial prudence means.

This was also my first experience of handling a team. I had Ayman, Javed and Jalil reporting to me and all were different characters.

- *My Eighth lesson learnt in GL was essentially my Saudi Experience and that was, Money and Work although Important, mental peace and security is equally important. Compromising for money is not worth the stress and it is better to let go of things making you uncomfortable than continuing to struggle*

- *My Ninth Lesson learnt was Discrimination exists globally and efforts have to be made to ensure you do not practice this in personal and professional life as it affects the person undergoing it very badly.*

My professional experiences with my colleagues taught me another important lesson. Till I went to Saudi, I always encountered colleagues in my limited space where they came in for some time and left.

By this I mean, as an Accountant in JL, I was supposed to get the information and compile them into the books, while in GLS, as a Project Budget's guy, project team used to come to me with their proposals, vouchers and contracts that I needed to review and approve them.

But in Saudi, although information was supposed to come to me, I was equally responsible to go out and collect them. So I had to enter into other domains to collect the information, like I needed to enter Sales Team Domain to collect information on what their projections for business were, enter the Project Team Domain to sit with them and look at their plans of when they will be getting their work done.

Nobody wants any person to enter their domains and if you are a person who not only has to enter the domain but also collect information, your task is more difficult, but my Saudi stint taught me how to do this.

- _My Tenth lesson learnt in GL was essentially the concept of Space and how, one needs to Respect it if one needs to make things happen._

I returned back to India after exactly 1 year 11 months. You will say I did not complete 2 years but I did technically, as I encashed my annual leave and clubbed it with EID. My departure to Saudi was dramatic from my point of view and my return from Saudi with a resignation in my hand was equally dramatic.

CN Sir is a great Business guy, very astute in judging people and based on his reading of people he knows how to utilize them to effectively get things done. Due to some misunderstanding with the management while returning back, I had decided to quit and even put in my paper, however CN Sir's maturity came forth and once I landed in Mumbai he asked me to meet him once before he would accept my resignation.

We had a nice chat in his cabin in E1 and he asked me one thing at the end of the meeting, "Would you like to work with me still?" to which I answered "Yes, Subject to you trusting me". After this he said only one thing "Forgot about everything and start working from tomorrow in my team".

After the discussion with CN Sir, I withdrew my resignation and joined back the Indian operations of NE. India operations had undergone various management changes by the time I returned to India. Captain had moved to a new group company as CFO, while AT Sir my boss in Saudi had become the new CFO of NE. CN Sir was being elevated to the group level and HKG Sir was being made the President of NE with OP as the Head HR for NE. By the time I returned AV Sir had also come back to India and a new set of project and support team were being developed.

I was appointed as the Contract Management person and designation given to me was Commercial Manager and my pay was the one I left India with, a princely sum of 12,718 net in hand. I did not argue and just joined back.

When I was returning back all of my other colleagues who were Commercial Managers like SD, TN and PJ were moving international with PP shifting along with Captain to the new group company.

In 2004, the Telecom Industry was the domain to be in due to its tremendous growth potential. Operators were rolling out the Networks and things were really looking good for the Telecom Sector in India. In 2004, Our Division had won 2 very big orders from NN India and NL India for rolling out the BSNL Pan India Network.

In those days winning a 90 crores deal was huge. Before this order the revenue of all NE operations across countries was around 100 crores and here were these orders which were each worth 90 crores. We had to roll out close to 2000 sites each for NN and NL and when I say roll out it means from physically constructing the site to civil and electrical work, installing all power and telecom equipment with finally getting all clearance. So essentially it was a full Turn Key Job.

I was appointed by AT Sir to look after NL Account while GG was appointed to the NN Account. I had AV Sir as the Project Director and there was CP Sir as NN Project Director. We had a relationship team as well which used to interact with the Customers and for NN there was SD Sir and for NL there was AG.

Since this was a good 2 year roll out, I thought it was a good opportunity and so readily picked it up. But again I did not know what I was getting myself into.

The first thing I did which I normally do even today is pick up the contract and read it, especially the fine print. After reading it, I went across to the Pre Sales team who had worked on the pricing and signing of the contract to understand exactly what our scope of work would be in this project as per them and map it to what is written in the contract.

Since, I was supposed to finalize the cost budget for the project team to follow, I also enquired about how the costing was derived by the Pre Sales Team. Initially there was some reluctance to share this information, but I was helped by SJ who made me understand the methodology used for arriving at the cost and then the price.

After understanding all aspects of the project which was my practice, I put things into a dashboard which would become my control sheet, remembering the training I got from CVK Sir with his dashboards. While I was making the control sheet and understanding the pricing, I realized there was something wrong in one of the assumptions taken and this assumption when looked at from the contract point of view would cost us heavily. From expected profit of 10%, we might end up incurring a loss on these projects. Instead of keeping quite as this was a big issue, I decided to share this inputs immediately with my seniors.

After discussions between the account management team, the project team and senior management, the only solution we all could come up with was that we would have to have a deep relook at how we would need to execute the project, as going back to the customer was not possible for upward revision in pricing.

The only way out of this situation being faced in the NN and NL project was working on a tight budget, accompanied by stronger negotiations with the suppliers and sub-contractors and trying to do as much work in house as possible. Accordingly a new cost budget was finalized and circulated.

Since the NL Project covered close to 8 states of India, starting from Karnataka, Andhra Pradesh, Kerela, Tamilnadu, in the South to West Bengal, Bihar, Jharkhand and Assam in the East, there was consensus between me and AT Sir that if we needed to control costs and ensure we monitor things effectively, we would have to follow a decentralized commercial structure as well, as was being implemented by AV Sir for projects.

The next month, I spent in recruiting my team across the location, from new hirers in Patna and Ranchi to realignment of existing resources within GL in other locations, to training them on my dashboard and how they needed to help me keep control on the cost elements of the project.

Once my team was in place and they were trained, I thought my work was 90% done, but as usual Balraj Sahani from "Waqt" had to come back in my life. I started getting calls from almost all states that the cost budget I had circulated to the project and my commercial team was not implementable.

Considering the field teams could not implement the cost budget and the situation in the field was becoming critical, it was proposed by the management that a core team of experts would be created who would go to the field and negotiate with the suppliers and sub-contractors and try and get things moving again. I was made a part of the team and again my travelling started.

The next two months were spent from one state to the other from one supplier to another from one sub-contractor to another. The team from HO managed to get the project work started and soon the field team took over as they saw that the cost budget could be implemented with a little extra effort.

To further control the project effectively AV Sir implemented a system of monthly reviews where the core team from each state would come down to HO and we would review the project thread bare from project issues to site issues to profitability at site level. Corrective actions were initiated immediately and all approvals put in place instantly.

This helped to keep us on track and ensured the lesson I had learnt from RJV Sir was perfectly true and correct. Decisions need to be taken on time and if you delay a decision it becomes irrelevant as something more complicated will come up which will make things worse. These reviews helped us execute the projects and ensure that we made money as well.

- *My Eleventh and Most Important Lesson was that one needs to use his learnings to succeed. The NL Project was one project which made me realise that whatever I learnt in JL in terms to speaking out, decision making and timings of decisions are the most important things.*

- *My Twelfth Lesson was it is important to set the example yourself when your team is getting stuck as it helps them to get unstuck*

Not all things were sailing smoothly though, the issue of how to step into someone domain and ensure the person whose domain you are entering, will cooperate with you still remained. Asking a team to work together is different than getting the team to work together.

The respect element one can ask people to follow but the respect has to come from within and it should not be superficial. The simple solution I used to solve this problem was, trusting my team and trusting them that they know their job and giving them space to make mistakes.

I still remember how my day used to start, invariably I would get a call from my field teams complaining about how the project team were not cooperating with them or AV Sir calling me and giving me an earful on how my commercial team members were not cooperating with his project guys on field.

The funny thing was both of the field teams were complaining on the same issue but to their respective bosses from their point of view, but the thing which helped us pull through this was although there were issues no one distrusted each other and there was respect for one another.

Then there were issues with the corporate accounts team whose job was to consolidate the data across all projects and submit it to the board and senior management for reviews.

The problem with the corporate accounts team and the commercial team was that we lived in two separate planets. Their methodology of preparing books and the way we reviewed project profitability at site level were totally different and this made it difficult to arrive at a common point and hence the conflict but somehow all of us managed to push through this as well as the element of Trust and respect remained.

- *My Thirteenth lesson learnt in GL was the Importance of Respect and Trust to take the team forward.*

GL Management helped me out a lot and just did not throw me under the bus. Once the Management realized that I was a good resource and could be developed as a future senior management member, I was recruited into the FJ program, under which a group of high performers were selected across GL and across functions.

This group was to be put under various development programs so that they could be groomed effectively for the future. Under this program I was put under two development programs, one with SP Jain Institute of Management and the other with IIM Ahmedabad. For a person who after the first month in college became an Outstanding Student, here I was attending classes and that too at some of the most prestigious institutes in India.

The experience in SP Jain and IIM was extremely good. It opened my mind further on how I can become a better manager and person. I remember the lectures of Dholakia Sir in IIM very clearly, the way he explained the structure of any economy and what is Macro Economics and what effect do policies have on economy are something which I cannot forgot. The way he summarized it was too good.

Along with Dholakia Sir, the Marketing Professor in IIM was also too good. He made me realize that when you interact with a customer, you need to put yourself in the mind-set of the customer.

Normally we go to a customer with what we want to say but forgot one important question, does the customer want to listen to what you want to say? So if you want your meeting with a customer to go off well, you need to first know what the customer wants to hear from your side and then you need to prepare yourself to say what the customer wants to hear?

This message was in a different way re-confirmed during another training program. We in our corporate world are told to standardize our presentation so that the message to the customer is consistent but in this standardization we forgot to answer the basic question does the Customer want to hear what you are saying?

The success of a meeting or a presentation is when the customer hears what he wants to hear from your side. When the right words come out of your mouth, the doors to future meetings get opened.

- *My Fourteenth lesson learnt through these training programs was One Size Does Not Fill All And Customization is the need of the hour*

These training programs helped me grow as a person.

I am sure when you look back at your work life; you will see some similarities to what I experienced. Your reactions would surely be different and similarly your learnings would also be different but you shall be able to correlate with at least some parts of my journey and this I am sure shall help you in identifying what your true beliefs are.

'Work is Important but Don't Forget to Live Life'

Chapter 9 - My Commandments

My experiences in JL and GL till now helped me come up with my Ten Commandments of Business which became my Belief System according to which I started working at my work place.

1. Say What Needs To Be Said No Matter How Bitter To Digest

2. Decisions Have To Be Taken And They Need To Be Based on Facts

3. Timings Of The Decisions Is The Most Important Decision One Needs To Take

4. Try And Remain Calm No Matter What And A Smile Goes A Long Way In Times Of Problems.

5. Keep Increasing Your Knowledge By Using The Formula 'L = P + S + P'

6. Always Be True To Your Core Beliefs and Priorities

7. Respect The Space Which The Other Person Occupies

8. Trust Your Colleagues, Seniors, Juniors

9. Understand That Each Person or Customer is different and Adapt Yourself Accordingly To Handle Them

10. Always Keep Moving Ahead

Similarly my experiences with my Elders, Cousins, Friends, School and Meeta, helped me to develop my Ten Commandments which became my Belief System for My Personal Life.

1. Keep Life Simple

2. Get Your Priorities Right

3. Be Mindful that Everyone in your Family is Different

4. Always be Respectful and Trust Your Family

5. Never Give Up No Matter What Happens On Your Family

6. Follow the KARMA Principal of Righteous Living and not the popular 'What Goes Around Comes Around One'

7. Never Compromise when it comes to your Family

8. Always plan for a rainy day

9. Always Find a Way To Move Ahead.

10. Keep Smiling and Be Happy And To Be Happy Use Your Memory Bank

You must have realized that every time I moved on, I never looked back. The reason why I do not like to look back is because I feel, I will not let go if I look back. It is difficult to explain, but I shall try.

I feel if I look back I shall be drawn to my old memories with a desire to live it again and again and if the others have moved on, I shall not be able to take it, so probably out of fear, I don't look back at all, thinking that as I have moved on others have too. This is one solution I use to keep moving ahead in life.

My fear of looking back has resulted in me being classified as a snob, as a person who is there for you only when he needs you. But the thing which I cannot do because of this fear of mine is going back to them to tell them, I am Sorry, I am sorry I was not in touch and the reason was not because I did not want to, the reason was because I could not. But hopefully once these friends of mine read these memoirs, they will at least realize that I have not forgotten any of them and I recollect all of them with a smile on my face and I am thankful to them for being a part of my life. This goes for all the people who have not been named also as my memories are so full of people writing them down would mean going on and on.

One more thing you would have noted, that I have nothing bad to say about anyone, probably I am being diplomatic or not being true to myself, but that is not the case. Another simple thing which I have done successfully is keep the bad memories of my life away from my good memories. I don't mix them up and because I don't mix them up, they don't trouble me on a day to day basis and that is why in my memories also they don't figure in my priority listing.

Once you have gone through my two sets of commandments you will find most of the commandments are very similar. At least the core essence remains the same between the two of them, which is, 'Respect, Trust and Always Trying to Move Ahead with a Smile'

Hopefully through your experiences in your life and through your various interactions with your Elders, Cousins, Friends, Spouses, you have your set of commandments developed.

I started this journey by telling you that one should prioritize and have a sizeable bank of good memories in one's life and when you combine this with your commandments; I can guarantee you that frustration shall go out of the window.

The value of my guarantee is however limited to 10% of the value of the book which you have bought.

My disclaimer is, 'Please do not follow my commandments as following them without arriving at your own shall invalidate this guarantee'

My testing formula for avoiding frustration from coming into my life was very simple as well and that was, 'the moment I start feeling frustrated with a decision I have made, or I cannot sleep, or I am generally unhappy, a bell rings in my head that tells me something is not as per my belief system and I need to course correct'.

My Journey with you however is not complete, as I need to share quite a lot with you in terms of the main aspect of my Commandments and that is how I implemented them, like it is said the 'The Proof Of The Pudding Is Eating It'. If I leave you here you will probably think I lived in an Utopian World and whatever I have said is all make believe and no one can succeed with such an idealistic belief system in today's world and I can't let you go thinking like that, can I?.

If you remember in the Chapter of Meeta, I have mentioned a few Challenges in everyone's life which needs management, which I am again stating below,

- Family Management

- Work Place Management

- Kids Management

- Society Management

Let's use this Analogy to take my story forward.

Chapter 10 - Family Management

First of All Remember my Ten Personal Commandments mentioned in the earlier chapter and then top that up with the below add-ons which Meeta and I came up together as they are primarily taken from Meeta's belief system as she insisted on it and you have the answer to the Million Dollar Question.

- Never Involve A Third Person In Our Problems

- Keep the communication channel open between us no matter how tough the situation between us becomes

- Try and Spend Some Personal Time with each other each day

- Try Smiling As Much As Possible (Shri Shri Ravi Shankar Ji also gives this as a solution for marital problems)

Out of all the commandments in a marriage or in a Family, the most important ones are Respect, Trust and Giving Time.

Everything else can be managed, but when Respect is lost, things go out of hand very quickly. Loss of Trust leads to insecurity and this opens the door for the Third Party to come in. Similarly in a Family, things cannot be rushed all the time as understanding one another is a continuous process and one needs to keep at it.

Like I have said 'The Proof of the Pudding is in eating it' and the proof that the above works is the way Meeta and I have used this to survive close to 22 years in our married life and in a family which as you know is very big and complicated. A few of the examples of tackling the problems faced are listed below,

CH-10.1 - The first trial of this solution we used to solve the Desi Ghee Problem.

Food at my place was cooked in Desi Ghee while Meeta hated the smell of Desi Ghee. Since she was new, she could not open herself up to my Mummy and tell her of this predicament.

I knew what Meeta was going through as she did confide in me, and the solution which we found for this predicament was a simple one, and that were "Evening Walks". Meeta and I would leave the house at 6:00 in the evening and come back by 7:30. The reasons for these walks were to spend some time and catch a quick bite as well. To keep my parents also happy we used to come back and eat a little more food with them, problem solved. So instead of losing weight on our walks we gained a few kilos.

This sub plot from our life was later borrowed by Akshay Kumar as a sub plot as well for "TOILET – A PREM KATHA", where the food issue was changed to the issue of Toilet. Luckily for me Meeta did not walk away from me because of this as was done by Bhumi Pednekar in the film.

After a few months when Meeta became a little comfortable in the house, Meeta did tell Mummy about her Desi Ghee issue and a solution was found that before adding the Desi Ghee, a portion of the ready food shall be kept aside for Meeta which would be without Desi Ghee.

We used 4 things from our list,

- First, Never Involved any Third Person,

- Second, respected the fact that Meeta had a problem.

- Third, tried to come up with a Solution to the best extent possible to keep things moving and buy time.

- Fourth, gave Time to my parents to accept Meeta.

CH 10.2 - The second set of problems we used this solution of ours to solve was when Meeta wanted to start working again.

Meeta wanted to start working after 6-8 months of marriage, but I asked her to take it slow for some time and once things with Daddy had stabilized as they had with Mummy, she could go and get herself a suitable job.

Daddy, however in one of his modern avatars in a family get-together said females should be allowed to work and make a career for themselves. This was the time Meghana was finishing her MBBS and Shweta was about to finish her Hotel Management degree.

Probably in hindsight it was me who was too scared to approach Daddy to seek his permission, probably it was all in my mind that Daddy would object, probably it was a figment of my imagination or probably it was because I could not open up to my father.

Meeta now took me up on this and said since Daddy does not have any issues with females working she would like to also go out and make a career for herself.

We had a long discussion during one of our evening walks and it was agreed between us that Meeta would get into Animation and Video Editing as she was not interested in pursuing any job which required her to use her Accounts background.

Since Animation and Video Editing was an upcoming field in those days (1998) and Meeta had previously done a programming course, Meeta herself felt that this would be something she would enjoy getting into. To pay the fees we decided to use our allowances and the money I was making from my part time job.

The way I convinced my parents was simple, since Shweta could study and then work, so could Meeta. The convincing worked as there could be no argument to this logic.

Once Meeta started working, problems were there, but decisions were not interfered in when it came to what Meeta wanted to do.

From working in SiBa Ads, to becoming a computer teacher in Saudi as well as in India later, to starting a catering business then again going back to teaching, to becoming a Student again, to becoming a Yoga Instructor. Meeta has tried it all after the initial hiccups.

To handle this situation we used 4 things from our list,

- First, Never Involved any Third Person

- Second, respected the fact that Meeta had a problem

- Third, tried to come up with a Solution to the best possible extent to keep things calm and moving

- Fourth, gave Time to my parents to accept Meeta's individuality

CH 10.3 - The Third set of problems we used this solution of ours to solve was when Meeta expressed a desire to experience life on her own.

Meeta had a rough pregnancy with Shreesh and an even worse one when we had Prithvi 10 years later, but when we were having Shreesh since all experiences were her first, Shreesh's pregnancy was more emotionally draining for her. She was put on bedrest for a major part of it and she had to give up her flourishing career as an editor and graphic designer with SiBa Ads. Not only did she manage to keep herself calm all through these issues, she also started eating things she would not dream of eating ever, all to keep the baby healthy.

From eating Karela's (Bitter Gourd) to Eating Raw Cabbages by the Kg's, she did it all. I saw a very different side, a very strong side of Meeta during this phase.

We had Shreesh when both Meeta and I were about to become 25. Shreesh was a healthy child but was premature by 4 weeks. Initial period was tough but since I was Ok with kids, handling Shreesh was not a problem. As I have said, give me a child and I can take care of them till the time they are hungry and that was my routine for the night.

Meeta too surprised me with her strength. Seeing Meeta I understood what being a Mother meant and what strength a woman gets when she becomes a Mother; Hats Off To All The Moms In The World.

Shreesh, being the first of his next generation and more closer to the age of my cousins, he was doted on by all my cousins and also by all my elders in the family. He was very cute as well. Karan, Tina, Ashish and Vipra were Shreesh's friends growing up along with Shashank, Shivek, Rohin and Rahul, the video skit which all of them performed in is truly hilarious.

Like I have said we are a crazy family when it comes to our relationship. Here was Shreesh who was the first of his next generation but he was just a year younger than my youngest cousin. Tinu Darling who is my cousin sister ties Rakhi to Shreesh. Like I said we are a crazy bunch.

Everything was sailing smoothing for some time. Meeta started becoming comfortable in the house with all the things. Daddy and Mummy too settled in as they too had a toy in the house to play with now. Daddy's insecurities were under control as well.

But then came, the issue with Rajesh my brother in law. My Daddy as an elder in the family gets involved and it is rightly said "When you don't understand the issue, you should not get involved". Things which were improving on Daddy and Mummy's front went from bad to worse. Nothing could be done on this issue. Neither I nor Meeta could do anything about it as this had nothing to do with us. Time being the best option to tide over this.

Another reason, which probably made Meeta express her desire to experience life on her own was because, living in a joint family takes away a lot of personal time which one needs and Meeta being an independent women wanted to experience freedom at least once, as by this time both Meeta and I had realized that the rest of our lives will be spent with my parents only as this was due to our upbringing.

Within a week of Meeta saying this, I got a call from CVK Sir who was my boss at that time in GL, asking me whether I would be interested in going to Saudi Arabia for a short period of time. These words seemed like magic to me. It seems here was Meeta making a wish and here was CVK Sir fulfilling it.

After a little bit of convincing my Daddy and Mummy that from a career point of view it was a good opportunity and after giving them an assurance, that they shall be seeing us almost every quarter and we shall be calling them almost every alternative day, they agreed to let us go.

There was however more resistance from Meeta's parents than mine. I remember how Meeta's Papa, used to call me or discuss with me when we met on why I am doing what I am doing i.e. going to Saudi Arabia of all places and that too with Meeta and Shreesh in toe.

Meeta and I not only met our commitments of calling our families regularly, but we also kept coming to India for every function or get-together to be with our parents and never defaulted on them. We even met our commitment of coming back within 2 years as we returned back after exactly in 1 year 11 months.

But through our vacations whether with our families or alone, I did show Meeta almost the entire world and we continued to spend some time alone from our parents to keep our minds fresh every year.

We also did a lot of activities during our trips for the very first time. From Scuba Diving to Snorkelling to Jet Skiing to Shark Diving to Bungee Jumping, to Annapurna Base Camp in a Helicopter to trek to Gaumukh, to going to the highest motorable road in the world, to the southernmost tip of Africa, to the river under the mountain in Philippines, to the sublime beaches of Maldives, to the amazing and beautiful outdoors in Sri Lanka, Myanmar and Nepal.

We have seen it all together. The only thing which I have not shown Meeta till date remains the Mumbai City where we live. This I have promised her, I shall show her when we become too old to travel the world, as local site seeing will be the only possible thing left for us to do together then.

We used 4 things from our list to handle this,

- First, respected the fact that Meeta's request was genuine

- Second, accepted what life threw at us with the knowledge that Life being simple is giving us an opportunity and we need to take it

- Third, Understood our Parents insecurities and promised we shall take care of it and made them understand our point of view as well

- Fourth, met our Commitments in terms to what we said to our elders and parents.

CH 10.4 - The Fourth set of problems we used this solution of ours to solve was moving out of our Hospital Building.

On our return from Saudi and after experiencing a society life surrounded by neighbours and friends, living in a Hospital environment was difficult.

But since I and Meeta were still reliant on my Father and his financial situation was only now improving, we did not want to burden him with our desire to move to an Apartment Complex so we kept quiet.

But when I got my salary revision from 12,000 to 52,000, the first thing we did was convince my father to invest in an Apartment which shall be paid off in EMI's which I shall service from my Salary and use the money I saved up in Saudi for the down payment, thereby drastically reducing the pressure on my Father.

By now my father had also realized that the hospital environment was not a suitable environment for his grandson and he agreed happily. We returned from Saudi in May 2004, bought the place in November 2004 and shifted in May 2005 and we have been staying happily here since then.

We used 3 things from our list,

- First, Respected my father's situation and only expressed our desire when we knew we were not burdening him

- Secondly, allowed time for my father to make up his own mind in terms of what was best for his grandson.

- Third, explained our point of view as well but respectfully

In our lives apart for the instances listed above, there were innumerable other challenges we faced, right from a miscarriage to when our second child Prithvi was born 8 weeks premature, my continuous Travel for close to 10-20 days in a month, Managing Family Dynamics. Life was full of up and downs but the one thing we continued and continue to do even today is move on as we never lost Respect and Trust for one another.

CH 10.5 - The Fifth and Most Important Set of problems – Surviving Each Other

We can talk, we can spend time with each other, we can respect and Trust each other, we can avoid involving third people in our problems, but will this suffice. I am sorry to tell you that it will not be so.

The one thing over and above the things already listed above which one needs to do is keep adapting to one another come what may.

I have already explained,

Adapting = My Actions,

Which means always being true to what you really are i.e. your belief system and doing things in the right sequence of your priorities.

The only way Meeta and I survived for so long was because somewhere our Priorities / Pillars were the same. The only part of our priorities which was different was Meeta was a Social Person and I was an Anti-Social Person and that is where majority of our tiffs centred around, as in her priority listing of personal time going out for parties came ahead of sitting in front of a TV watching a movie or a match.

But we managed to overcome these issues as Meeta valued her peaceful sleep more than Socializing. Meeta had to become Anti-Social like me because of me, but she decided to adjust only because of my ability to put Meeta to sleep, which was unsurmountable.

My voice had and still has a calming effect on Meeta. Even when she used to cry and I used to try to calm her down by speaking to her, she invariably slept off. She even sleeps off now, when I speak to her for too long. This is probably one of the main reasons for our marriage continuing to go ahead in full steam.

I know some of the examples listed by me as challenges are not even challenges in the real sense, but each of these issues needed to be managed and all I wanted to tell you is that even silly issues can be managed through your belief system, since silly issues could be managed, bigger issues were a cake walk for us.

Surviving a marriage especially in a Joint Family set up, is all about knowing who you are and who your partner is and who your parents and other family members are and handling them in a manner where you are always true to yourself as a person.

Not easy but if you are looking at the right places for the answers and know this formula and have your list of commandments in place, I guarantee you that you shall be successful.

The value of my guarantee is however limited to 10% of the value of the book which you have bought.

My disclaimer is, 'Please do not literally take my solutions and follow it blindly, but come up with your own special ones'

Chapter 11 - Work Place Management

Whenever you join any organization, all your efforts should go in learning, learning how things work in that organization, seeing where you fit in, spending time in understanding your juniors, colleagues, seniors, looking at how you can contribute to your organization and above all always being True to yourself.

Being artificial only takes you a few steps forward but if you are in for the long haul, you need to be yourself to succeed.

You need to spend some personal time as well developing your commandments which are based on your life and your belief system.

We being lazy animals, we start thinking we can copy someone else's commandments and fit that in our lives and become successful and hence the books of renowned successful people are the best sellers in today's business world.

We don't realize that although guides are good, but you need to write your own paper to succeed and no two lives are the same and without understanding that we just blindly start following them.

We need to learn from our great minds, but we need to make our own paths and that is what we keep forgetting and that is why my dear friends only 1% of the population of the world own 90% of the wealth of the world.

So you will ask me a question, Why I am writing all this stuff?

Well Friends, I am writing this stuff, because I was bored during the 8 weeks of lockdown and had no other work and I thought you might get bored in the future as well, as I am told Corona Virus is not going away from our life for a long time to come and therefore you will also have a lot of time to read this book, just kidding my friend, just kidding.

I am writing this book because I wanted to write it from a perspective of a person who in a classical sense is a no one. A person who has only tried to live a life in a manner which he thought was right and I have no expectation from this book that anyone reading this book will get inspired or anything. Being an introvert, putting myself in front of the world is my final step in opening up and that is what I am doing by writing this book.

Continuing my story ahead…..

There is a term in modern management, being Professional, which according to me simply means 'I have a Personal Life which is different from my Work Life and I don't mix the two'. In the guise of Professionalism, I have seen innumerable people forgetting they have a personal life and I have also seen innumerable people mixing their personal and professional life.

Once you have worked long enough and developed your Commandments based on which you would like to work, you need to implement your thoughts in your action.

In my case, my growth story up to the time I become CFO was all about learning and unlearning and developing my

Commandments and my life after becoming CFO was again learning, learning how to survive the challenges which came my way using my commandments.

CH 11.1 - How I Overcame My Merger Dilemma

Till I became the CFO in 2008 of NE, whatever challenges I faced were comparatively very small and related to work which everyone knew needed to be done and therefore was under one's control. It was only when I become CFO of NE in 2008 that I realized what it meant to be a part of the management team and what all goes in the corporate world at the higher levels.

In case of NE Division the growth was phenomenal. From a small office in Pune in 1999 doing BTS Installation, NE had grown big with operations in close to 40 countries by 2008.

When an organization grows the first thing which grows along with it are the processes and that is what happened with NE. Earlier no one looked at NE Division but by 2008, everyone was noticing it and here I was in the middle of it.

GL had separate accounts team for each division and then a corporate team doing the consolidation. By 2008 all other divisions had shut shop and only NE remained with a Turnover of close to 2,500 Crores. So it was logical that to cut cost the two functions should be merged.

A small task force team was formed who was supposed to propose the new support organization structure along with roles and responsibility of this new organization. After a couple of months of discussion there were 2 sticking points which we members could not agree upon, the first being who shall lead the team in the state and to whom will the field team report to at the centre.

I was of the opinion it should be the senior most person who is also the most qualified in the state who should lead the team and this head shall report back to me as Deputy CFO Projects and me in turn shall report to the Group CFO. The Group CFO shall have another Deputy CFO who will be responsible for Accounts and Balance Sheet Preparation.

MB Sir, who was also a member of the task force and my senior, was of the opinion it should be the Accountants in each location irrespective of seniority or suitability who should lead it and the field team should report back to the Deputy CFO who was looking after Accounts and Balance Sheet Preparation and with me working as Projects CFO.

My logic for the proposal was simple, since I was responsible for Projects, I needed the field teams to report in to me as how else would I control the financials of the projects in the field as that was the only thing happening in the field. As for the accountants leading the state I was Ok with it at the locations they were the senior most and qualified.

MB Sir, being an accountant and an excellent one with phenomenal hold and understanding of Balance Sheets and its preparation, looked at everything from an accountant's prism; hence his suggestions were guided by his understanding.

If I had accepted MB Sir's view, there was no role left for me as without a team to lead what good was I as the Deputy CFO Projects. This issue became a stalemate as in spite of the

Management and all senior colleagues of mine intervening, this stalemate could not be broken.

In one of our review meetings, our group MD even proposed sending me and MB Sir on an Island alone to sort this issue out.

Seeing this going nowhere and probably since I was in a more secure zone, I decided to quit GL and was ready to put in my papers to get a resolution to this problem as I needed to be True to myself and my beliefs.

With this episode, when I look back, I can reflect on another Hypothesis I developed during another IIM Workshop I attended.

As per this new Hypothesis, which I repeat "PLEASE DO NOT TAKE SERIOUSLY", we Humans love living in a homogenous environment, if however we come across someone or something which threatens to break this homogeneity, we fight it back.

Initially, we fight through discussion to convince them to again rethink their positions and if they still continue on the path of thinking differently, we then threaten to throw them out of our group and even if this does not work then the majority destroys them entirely to protect their homogeneity.

Why I am saying this episode of mine takes me to this hypothesis is because after I moved out, the structure as I had proposed was implemented with a Group CFO, with the Field Teams Reporting to the Deputy CFO Projects and there being a separate Deputy

CFO for Accounts and Balance Sheet Preparation. The rest is for you to conclude as to who was not the homogenous element.

I used the below things from my Commandments to handle this situation,

- First, Say what needs to be said no matter what the consequences are.

- Second, Decision has to be taken and if no one is taking one, you need to step up and take it instead of lingering on.

- Third, Manage to remain Calm.

- Fourth, Be true to yourself and your priorities.

- Fifth, Try and find a solution to how you can keep moving ahead.

CH 11.2 - How I Overcome The Challenge of Moving from Back Office To Front Office In GL

Now you will think when I first came across a problem, I immediately quit and left GL. My dear friends that was not the case, the decision of stepping aside was just the first step in the right direction as my belief of whatever happens, happens for your best was to kick in.

CN Sir being an astute judge of person thought I could be used effectively on the Sale side if not on the Finance Side and therefore proposed for me a role of Pre Sales Head responsible for developing a Centralized Pre Sales Team which would support the various geographies were NE had operations.

Since this was a new challenge and me being me, I decided to take it up.

A small pre-sales team was already in existence in GL and I replaced JR who was heading it previously as JR moved to UK to join Project Operations there.

While I was handling the Pre Sales Function, I took my first decision which resulted in an actual loss to the company. Since the function of Pre Sales had a mandate of centralizing the costing and sales offerings across the globe, I and my team invested in a software, which we thought would help us to track all offers made across the globe and would also help in generating offers itself as costing is all about breaking down the scope into activities and costing the activities.

We worked hard for it but when it came to implementation, none of the International Locations wanted to comply with it on the grounds that, how can someone in India know the situation on the field and customer negotiations is very dynamic and there cannot be a to and fro all the time.

The lesson I learnt with this failure was simple, there is tremendous resistance when you want to change something. The management of GL was kind enough to overlook this loss I had incurred as I was not to blame 100% for it and still continued to back me.

Nepal became my first test bed and because of the sole efforts of SH from my team, SD Sir and MR from Sales supporting SH, we managed to win a huge order. There was however scepticism across NE as to how we shall execute this project as the last time we tried executing a project in Nepal, we had failed miserably.

At this point of time I don't know what came over me but I put my neck on the chopping board and said, we can execute the project as I and my team had studied all aspects of the deal and it was implementable.

Even CN Sir was sceptical about we being able to deliver and I remember the conversation which I had with him where he said "Anup, you are taking a very big risk with this, Are you Sure?" to which I said "Yes". He asked this question to SH as well and luckily he also said yes.

By this time the concept of a Centralized Pre Sales was not working and since I had stuck my head out for chopping on the Nepal order, CN Sir and the entire Senior Management team thought it was best to give me the entire responsibility.

Since apart from Nepal there were two small operations in Bangladesh and Sri Lanka, they gave me charge of these two countries as well and made me the Regional Director, responsible for these countries.

From Back Office to Now Full Front Office in one year, by end of 2008, I had moved from being the CFO for Network Engineering Division to being Regional Director – Nepal, Bangladesh and Sri Lanka Operations.

Coming back to my Management since they were taking a bet on me, they said I would not be given an increment nor any special privileges and my position shall be reviewed after a year based on my performance.

I agreed to all their conditions but put three conditions from my side. First being, my base location shall be Mumbai, Second being, I shall form a small core team who will help me develop and monitor the operations based out of Mumbai and finally, I shall have a say in the development of operations teams in each of the countries.

The management probably thought my chances of failing were exceptional bright and therefore readily agreed to my conditions.

I used 4 things from my commandments here,

- First, when an opportunity knocks and shows you a path through which you can keep moving ahead, you need to take it.

- Second, Learn and Adapt to what is thrown at you

- Third, Trust your team when they tell you it can be done and support them

- Fourth, Be True to yourself

CH 11.3 - How I Overcame The Challenges of Delivering on My Commitments in Nepal, Sri Lanka and Bangladesh

By 2009, the merger of all support functions happened and with NE Division no longer in existence, HKG Sir was moved to another Group Company while SK Sir came in his place as COO of GL. My reporting changed to SK Sir and remained so for the next 10 years.

Now that you know I survived for 10 years, you would have realized that I was able to deliver on my commitments to the management. But the story of me being able to deliver was again one hell of a ride.

Nepal Operation was to be set up from scratch, right from recruitment of Sales to Project to Support, to selection of office, guest house, and to set up of the company, everything needed to be done.

My small team comprising of SH, RM, MM ji and few others however were fully charged up. There was a vision which we all agreed upon and that was to make these 3 countries highly successful.

A number was agreed between us and that was 25 Mn USD (100 crores INR at the currency rate in 2008) which according to us will mean success to us. It was an ambitious number as when I took over, Bangladesh was doing around 1 Mn USD yearly with Sri Lanka doing around 1-2 USD Mn yearly and Nepal just starting.

Depending on what was needed we split our responsibilities, SH and RM went to Nepal for recruitment and operations set up with me handling Company formation, MM looked after developing Bangladesh through his contacts which he had developed during his stint earlier in Dhaka and since Sri Lanka operations already had a full-fledged team in place, I would look after increasing the business in Sri Lanka through the existing team.

Every step was a challenge in Nepal but we somehow managed

to survive for the first year in spite of everything which could go wrong, going wrong.

Initially, I was new to the roll of Business Head and I relied on my seniors to guide me. I selected resources that were recommended to me as I was too new to say no. I also agreed on a back end support structure to support the field operations.

All of which I should have not. But luckily for me, I corrected myself.

After 6 months of project starting, I went across and expressed my displeasure to the management on the resources deployed and requested for a free hand to deploy few strong resources which had been identified by me because of past experiences with them, to get the situation back in control.

On the support side also, I insisted that payment delays cannot be tolerated in Nepal and there should be a system in place, were based on my approval payments shall be released immediately with me taking 100% guarantee for its accuracy.

Luckily for me, Management agreed to my requests. Another reason for agreeing to this was we had already received close to 1 Mn USD as advance payment from the customer and now there was no going back.

SH along with GG, were deployed initially to handle the customer issues of delivery and GG and SH were given a free hand to change field teams as they deemed fit. This worked wonders as with payments getting streamlined and field delivery improving, the customer issues were resolved to a great extent. In the meantime, a Country Head was also selected and this time from outside GL as I by now knew I had to start saying no to recommendations if they did not suit my requirements.

Accordingly, VSR joined me in 2009 and he has been one of the few outsiders, who succeeded in GL. I also transferred JD from Sri Lanka to replace GG and SH and also got JS transferred from Indonesia to look after Accounts as I had got the company formation part also completed by 2010 and succeeded in delinking Nepal completely from India.

By the time we finished this order, thanks to the efforts of SH and GG and the new team, not only did the end customer appreciate our delivery but also gave us a direct order for roll out and later on for maintenance as well.

In Bangladesh, with the help of MM Ji, we were able to revive the operations. Another good decision we took was to get people who had previous experience of Bangladesh coming back to join our team, whether it was AG in Accounts and Finance or JK in Delivery. The only change I did was Sales as I localized my sales team with a Bangladeshi CEO and his Sales Manager. A gap I had identified during my experience in GL previously.

Another thing that was firstly initiated by me and executed successfully was the Customer Meet, a first of its kind. When I took over as the Regional Director, the first thing I noticed in Sri Lanka and Bangladesh was, although we were a successful company in India, the end customer in Bangladesh and Sri

Lanka which in our case were the operators did not know anything about us.

To enable them to see who we are I convinced SK Sir to allow me to organize a one of its kind Customer meet with invitation being sent to all CXO's of the Operator in each country.

After initial scepticism, this was allowed with a condition that this cost shall be part of the budget already signed off. I agreed and we had our first CXO Conference.

The responsibility of getting the CXO's on Board was given to the Country Heads who by now were in place. Since this was their first assignment and it was mentioned they would be reviewed on this, we were able to get at least one CXO Level person from each operator in Nepal, Sri Lanka, Bangladesh, Bhutan and Maldives coming to our conference which was planned in Sri Lanka.

It was going to be a one day conference in Colombo with a two night stay at Bentota for local site seeing in Sri Lanka. All expenses being borne by GL.

Luckily the conference went off well with one of the highlights of the session being the discussion which happened between the CTOs of an Operator from Bangladesh and Maldives, CEO of An Operator in Bhutan, SK Sir and AV Sir from GL. We organized another conference the next year but this time in Maldives.

This conference was a bigger success as after the Sri Lanka Conference the word had gone back that the conference organized by GL was conducted well and the discussions were informative and Maldives as a destination also had a big part to play in attracting the customers. From a count of around 12 in Sri Lanka, we were able to attract close to 43 CXO Level Resources in Maldives. Now with access to the senior most management of the End Customers a lot of doors opened for us.

The doors opened, but orders were won only on merits with solution and pricing playing an important part in it.

One thing I implemented across all my countries of operation was how revenue would be booked. The entire focus was on completing the works and getting the sites invoiced as soon as possible.

The reason I did this was because I had understood by now that if I needed my countries to succeed they needed to be financially independent and the only way this would be achieved would be by following financial prudence across the board. Cost budgets were prepared for each project; budgets allocated to each department and were reviewed on a regular basis.

With financial prudence and access to key decision makers, our business grew across all countries. From a small country like Nepal and Bangladesh we managed to start clocking consistently a revenue of around 10 Mn USD yearly each, with Sri Lanka and Maldives doing 5 Mn USD.

Since, I believed in cash I ensured at least a portion of the cash profit earned was transferred back to GL in the form of dividends and only the amount required for managing 3 months of working capital retained back for future contingencies.

I being me also realized that each country has a capacity in terms of revenue they can generate and therefore immediately on settling the operations in Nepal, I tried looking at newer geographies we could expand in. Another reason for looking for newer geographies, was the confidence in SH and my team to set up another country as we had set up Nepal.

In the initial phase we looked at Afghanistan and I did have a few preliminary discussions but the resistance from GL Management was too high and we finally settled for Myanmar as the country we would look at for expansion. The only thing I did was I created separate teams who would look at this expansion phase.

I again put my head on the chopping board and decided to invest in setting up Myanmar operations from any surplus I generated from optimizing costs of operations in my countries. This being a Win-Win for the management as they had nothing to lose but everything to gain, they decided to allow me to progress on my highly optimistic plan. The story of Myanmar Operations I shall touch base later.

Across all my geographies the one thing I ensured was that everyone knew what my expectations from them were at the same time I never interfered in the day to day operations of my Country Heads.

There is a saying that on a ship there can be only one captain and for me that captain at the country level was the Country Head.

I ensured the Chain in command was followed always. Even if I had to reprimand a Country Head for their performance, I tried to do it one on one and never in front of his team.

My logic for doing this came from my core belief system that Respect is important for developing Trust and since the country head needed his team to trust him, I never wanted the country head to lose respect in the eyes of the team he was supposed to lead.

Another thing which probably helped me in this phase was that although whatever I implemented had been done before, all I did was customize it for me and my team's needs.

I used almost all my Commandments during the challenges I faced in setting up Nepal, Bangladesh and Sri Lanka Operations and making them successful.

- First, never shy away from saying what needs to be said, even if it means admitting your mistakes.

- Second, take decisions when they are needed to be taken

- Third, take decisions which are based on facts and not based on any assumptions. e.g. Delivery was not happening and hence team needed to be changed

- Fourth, Remain Calm when things are not going our way

- Fifth, Be true to your core belief of transparency and trusting your team

- Sixth, Respect your team and give them the space to deliver

- Continuously keep the learning curve going as the experiment with CXO conference taught me

- Continuously keep thinking of how you can keep moving your team forward

But I also added something to my commandments and my learnings and that were.

- 'Every Team requires a goal, a tangible goal to achieve'. The most important element of this goal setting is that it should be achievable and within the capabilities of the team.

- Another important lesson is if you want to lead a team you need to ensure you take the risk element on yourself and not on your team members.

- Once the goal has been achieved, you need to give time to the team to enjoy their achievements.

- You need to take care as to the timing of how you put forth the next target in front of your team to immediately push on.

- Another Lesson I learnt was on how insecurities plays an important role in how people take decisions. It is when insecurity overcomes you that the logic part goes out of the window.

- Another learning I had was insecurity has another effect on people and that is why they lose the power of decision making. It is very easy to convince an insecure person to allow you to take a decision as all an insecure person wants is an escape path, an escape path that can tomorrow be used to fend off any liabilities which might accrue if things go wrong. Like it is said insecurities are highest at the top and the rest is for you to interpret.

CH 11.4 - How My Team Overcame The Challenges of Surviving the Telecom Bust

By 2012, Nepal, Sri Lanka and Bangladesh Operations had stabilized and we were executing a small project in Maldives as well. I was also helping GL Management with another set of issues which were there in other APAC Countries because of an acquisition which was done in the past. The reason probably I was asked to step in and head the APAC operations as well was because I had helped out during the acquisition of the company and had experience of the business they did.

As a first step as what has been my normal practice, I met up with the teams in each country and communicated the plan which was approved by the management to them.

As per the plan we closed down Thailand and Vietnam Operations while focussing on growing business in Indonesia and Philippines. The Indonesia and Philippine teams were given their targets after discussing with them and I started working closely with them.

The next 2 years that is 2012 to 2014 were spent between Nepal, Bangladesh, Sri Lanka, Indonesia and Philippines. I literally started living out of a suitcase, spending close to 20-25 days a month in these countries.

There was a joke going around within my friends and family circle that to meet me one needs to visit me at the airport. I travelled so much that I used to fill up the Jumbo Passport booklet within 12-15 months. My US Visa which I got in 2009 is now 5 jumbo passports old is how much I travelled.

Because of the cancellation of the Telecom License by the Supreme Court in 2012, the Telecom Industry had gone into a tail spin in India. Capex spending by Operators by 2013 drastically reduced and each operator was looking at optimizing cost.

As a result the Indian Operations of GL was badly affected and since India operations was the parent for all international subsidiaries, investment in developing newer geographies or investment in existing geographies drastically reduced. Any proposal requiring investment was to be approved at times from the board as well and that started becoming a big bottleneck as bankers came on the board.

The plan for expanding and growing business was now off the table, with the focus being on conserving cash. Luckily for me I had anticipated this and with the support of my local team we had managed to isolate our operations in Nepal, Bangladesh and Sri Lanka by making them financially independent with a decent year on year Revenue and with a habit of always being Cash Positive. But since I had just taken over Indonesia and other operations in APAC, I did not get enough time to work with the local teams there to build their financial independence.

Unfortunately in 2014, I was jolted by 2 more incidents which shook my core belief system.

The First shock came from Sri Lanka, where based on my Trusting nature, I was unable to judge my Country Head and I relied on the words of the customer which they had personally given me. The words of the country head of Sri Lanka which he told me while quitting summarized his insecurity "You will go away from here, but I need to stay and live here".

This he said because he did not want to take up the legal fight with the Customer who had defaulted on his commitments as he knew the fight would be bitter and even if we won or lost, he would lose his friends in the government and telecom industry and Sri Lanka being a small market, he could not afford to do so.

Till this incident I thought Trust and Respect is the only thing which matters in a team but after this incident, I realized there is another important element to this equation and that is the mind-set of your team members.

The feelings and insecurities an individual faces in his personal or professional life is equally important when you are driving a team forward to achieve the goals set forth.

This aspect of a person's mind-set has been summarized in an excellent paper titled "Lost to Frankenstein Detail: The Unravelling and Salvaging of Strategy from the wonderland of Pixies, Goblins, Angels and Santa Claus" written by Ajeet Mathur of IIM Ahmedabad. I am still in contact with my old Country Head of Sri Lanka but all through the legal battle which lasted for a good 3 years with the end customer, the former country head never once stepped forward to help us out.

The second shock came from Bangladesh, from the actions of my Country Head again who was from a finance background and whom I had hand-picked initially to head the Accounts and Finance Function and later elevated to Country Head. It was a minor issue, but I still went ahead with reliving him.

We did not part on any bad note; I sat down with him and explained that I am taking this action because of two reasons; one being his health which had deteriorated very badly over the last year and second the trust element had disappeared. The Country Head and me are still in touch and do catch up personally but from that date onwards, I have not worked professionally with him.

The above two shocks shook me up from inside as till this point of time in my professional career I had never encountered insecurities and trust issues. But this was certainly not the last time I encountered them.

I have lost my cool quite a few times on my colleagues and at times my superiors as well, but as soon as I have lost my cool I have also managed to get it under control very soon thanks to my formula that if I feel bad about something, then it must not be good and immediately I would course correct and go across to the other party and express my regret on losing control over myself. This greatly helped me keep my team with me inspite of my occasional outbursts.

GL by 2014 was deep in trouble with share prices crashing, debts mounting up and cost cutting happening across the board. Managing to retain talent was becoming difficult as there was no growth which was coming through.

Amidst this gloom, came the news that our efforts in Myanmar were about to pay off. After investing close to 150,000 USD from the optimized costs of Nepal, we were about to receive our first order in Myanmar. But instead of there being cheers to our efforts, the first statement which came from the management was "We cannot help you out". Here again there were only two choices in front of us, either allow our 4 years efforts to be washed away or come up with a solution in which we would not be needing any support from our Corporate.

We chose the latter and through a local partner in Myanmar arranged a financial arrangement under which he would invest and apart from being paid interest on his investment, he shall take a profit share as well.

Convincing GL Management was easy as they had nothing to lose and everything to gain. Since all our operations across countries were also struggling, starting Myanmar Operations was a wise decision as we could divert good talent to Myanmar to ensure we could deliver effectively to our customers.

The most important part of the deal with the local partner was that it was purely based on trust, he trusting me and SH that we would deliver on our words and commitments. The local partner ended up lending us close to 6 Mn USD, but because of SH and the team in Myanmar we not only delivered to the customer but also repaid the entire loan of 6 Mn back to our partner along with interest and also gave him a sizeable share in the profit earned. Even GL management got a sizeable share in the profits without any investment and with zero risk.

This solution became our biggest problem as well as every time it came to investments going forward, me and SH were asked to find out a partner who would invest the way YPH our partner had done. But unfortunately you get good people only once in a while and we could never manage anyone similar.

The fight which I had with the management to allow SH to become the country head can be shared with you'll some other time, but it makes me feel very proud seeing the success which SH has achieved as he was the only guy who never said no to any work. Give him a task and 9 times out of 10 it shall be done to 100% of your satisfaction.

There was a saying I used to say to my team, that one needs to bet on the best horse if one has to win the derby. By betting on the best horse, my references were towards the resources. It is only when you select the right resources one can succeed, so always try and look out for talent and when you spot talent, then give them the opportunity to grow, do not stifle them.

Like what I did in Nepal, I let SH lead the team without my interference; he was the captain of the ship and with me stepping in only when I felt the things were going off track.

Myanmar was another country which was set up from scratch like Nepal but keeping the same guidelines of financial prudence in mind and the focus was on getting the relationship developed at the End Customer Level. It was in Myanmar where the OEM actually felt threatened by us, but that is another story for some other time.

I and SH often joke about what would have happened if we had failed to repay the 6 Mn we had borrowed from YPH our local partner in Myanmar, as we had realized by now GL would not be extending any help.

I got to make a whole new set of friends in Myanmar and connect with a few old ones as well. Like Nepal, the group which was created in Myanmar was a terrific bunch, from Garg Sir, to Takane Sir, to Mahesh, to RM, to Anuj to Mithun, to KD to LN, to Anupam, to Pandu, to Hiten, to Pramod, to Sujith, to Sharni, to Ratish, to MD, to Ashwin, to Suu, and many more, they were just too good.

It was in 2015, owing to the financial crisis being faced, it was decided by the Board of GL to shut all non-profit companies across the world and all companies below 5 Mn USD revenues. The loss making companies were closed to preserve cash while smaller companies were closed to ensure cash could be deployed to countries with higher potential to become 10-20 Mn turnover companies, like US and UK.

Fortunately for me, Nepal and Myanmar were contributing above the threshold so they qualified to be continued, but other geographies did not and they needed to be closed down as per management directive.

I understood the logic for the decision and agreed to close down all operations except Indonesia, which I felt had the potential to become a 10-15 Mn revenue generating company. But however hard I tried, I was not able to convince my management in spite of the fact that a huge order of close to 10 Mn was in the pipeline and almost on the verge of closing.

So from being the Regional Director of close to 9 Countries, I was left with just 2 countries namely Nepal and Myanmar by 2017.

However, the revenue contribution did not shrink. We continued to contribute 25-30 Mn USD every year to the corporate cause with profit in the double digits in percentage terms.

Apart from closing down companies in my geography, I was also asked to look into Saudi and Dubai operations closures. For Saudi again Anna was attached to me while for Dubai, it was me and PJ my auditor friend who worked on it.

As part of the process of closure, I needed to spend time in Dubai as well working with the teams to close projects and collect the money due.

During this phase, I learnt a good lesson that in spite of your best efforts there are somethings which are beyond your control and it is best you let go of them.

Another important lesson learnt again was if you find something is going wrong or you have made a mistake, it is in your best interest to own up to it and take corrective action. Shying away from a decision will do you more harm, so take the decision and correct the situation.

I was tested during this phase to the fullest as although there was success in the form of Myanmar Operations being successfuly set up but at the same time there was failure as I needed to close down 7 country operations. The commandments I used to tide over this phase were,

- First, never shy away from learning and taking up newer challenges

- Second, Adapt to the changing scenarios, you cannot assume things will remain the same all the time and there is no harm in taking a step back to ensure things can keep going

- Third, Remain Calm when things are not going our way

- Fourth, Be true to your core belief of transparency and Trust your team

- Fifth, Respect your team and give them the space to deliver

- Sixth, Continuously keep thinking of how you can keep moving your team forward

- Seventh, Understand each and every member in your team are different and they might have their own insecurities and belief systems which drives their decisions.

CH 11.5 - How I Overcame My MOVING ON Dilemma

My team and I had realized that if we needed to continue to be financially independent then it could only be possible with moving to other sectors or expanding ourselves.

Power and IT which included Data and Call Centres were

shortlisted by my team to be the potential revenue drivers beyond 2016 and accordingly we had put a small team in place to look at developing these sectors.

Unfortunately, since the financial bandwidth was not there, we could not progress on this much and with Management constraints on getting newer partners coming on board; the plans remained on paper because none of these expansions plans were possible without getting on board newer partners who could either bring in the required credentials or capital.

Till 2016, I used to spend close to 10-15 days every month outside India, which I increased to 20 days, when the management requested me for spending more time in my countries. But the one thing I was consistent about was come what may I shall spend at least a week to ten days in Mumbai with my family. I did this consistently since 2008, when I took over as a Regional Director.

Another reason I did not like spending time in the geographies beyond 7-10 days is because I did not want to undermine what I had worked hard for and that was to make my Country Heads the Captains of the ship.

According to me 7 to 10 day period was enough in each country as I would spend 1-2 days reviewing with my country head and his team the performance of the past month and working on the plans for the coming months and 1-2 days spent in meetings with customers and 1-2 days going across to regional offices or conducting training workshops. This way the team in the country knew that there was someone watching them and supporting them at the same time.

With me being around all the time, it would have resulted in me subconsciously taking over as I would then have people coming to me for all sorts of issues, the ones previously which the country head handled and I would end up undermining my own country head by getting involved and that is one thing I never wanted to do.

The most difficult thing a leader needs to learn is sometimes it is good to let go, let go for others to take charge, let go for others to get the job done than doing it all the time yourself.

By the start of 2017-2018, things started deteriorating not only within GL but overall in the Telecom Sector across the globe. Operators were pulling back their capex plans drastically, owing to their own financial constraints, which was resulting in our business shrinking as well.

In 2016-2017, GL management came up with a plan for International Subsidiaries to be segregated from GL India and hived off in to a separate subsidiary. This was being done to enable new investors to come on board. To implement this plan a new team was formed under SK Sir to work with all Regional Directors. A new brand was being looked at also for this new segregated entity.

Since I had handed over all my daily responsibilities to my Country Heads and since expansion plans were also put on the backburner, I started interacting with the new team formed and helping them to understand how we operate and the challenges we face.

I was and I am still a very transparent person, everyone in my team and management, knows what I am thinking and doing as I don't shy away from saying what I feel is right. In 2017, a family decision was taken to re-develop a small plot of land which my father and my uncle owned and commercially exploit it. I did not hide the fact that when I was in India spending time with my family, I would be working on the re-development of the farm which Meeta would handle once it was completed.

This re-development however never came in the way of my support to the country operations and I continued to spend close to 15-20 days a month in Nepal and Myanmar working with the teams. After 2017, since there were no investments coming through still from the management, I used the time I was spending in the countries to interact with the teams more from a mentoring than a boss perspective.

Since the team below the Project Manager level were mostly fresher's with hardly any work experience, I started mentoring them on the basics of communications both external and internal. With Project Managers, I started working on making them understand financial prudence. With Senior Managers I started discussing how they need to understand strategy formulations and how their behaviour should be when representing the company and above all what should be the ethics with which one should drive the team.

Probably, subconsciously I was doing what all my bosses and colleagues had done with me and that was passing on their knowledge to me, right from RJV Sir, HD Sir, to KK Sir, to SN

Sir, to CVK Sir, to Captain, to AT Sir, to CN Sir, to HKG Sir to SK Sir to PJ to DB, to AG, to SH, to VSR, to JD, to SH, to KD, to OP, to Anna, to MM, to PG, to AB, to MB, to BK, to SJ, to YPH, to everyone I came in contact with.

In 2018 another issue came up and that was pertaining to a slew of bad publicity which GL received and almost all our customers panicked in terms of our existence.

Even our field teams were being called by our customers to find out if we would continue our operations and these calls created a crisis situation in the field.

To stem this crisis, it was agreed between me and my Country Head that I would be travelling to all field locations to interact directly with the team and assure them of there being no truth in the rumours being spread about GL. During the end of 2017 and 2018, I met the entire 300-350 people who were working on projects in Nepal and Myanmar. Times were tough but we still managed to achieve revenue of 8 Mn USD in Nepal and around 18 Mn USD in Myanmar in 2017-2018.

The situation in 2018-2019 also remained the same with revenue ranging in the same levels. But since this meant stagnation, there was tremendous pressure from the senior management. There were numerous rounds of meeting with to and fro data flowing, but since me and the country teams knew what we were talking about when it came to potential business possibility from Nepal and Myanmar our numbers were not changing.

With facts we communicated that Telecom as an Industry was struggling in our geographies and the only way we could increase our top line was by expanding our operations both geographically and in sectors.

In 2018, it was agreed that we should start exploring again and the management was ready to fund this expansion. Accordingly efforts were made in Nepal to get into Data Centre set up and in Myanmar into Call Centre and Logistics Business.

I always believed it is a team that shall deliver and not an individual and therefore after getting the go ahead from the management to expand, a team was created with the support of the Country Heads for each on these expansions plans.

Partners in Nepal were identified who could work with us in Data Centre set up, in Myanmar a logistics team was created whose job was to identify potential partners to tie up with and get this business rolling. Me and SH even travelled to US to meet a Tower Company and see if deployment as a service could be launched in US.

All these initiatives to materialize first of all needed investments and then time to gestate and start delivering in terms of Revenue and Profitability.

There was a saying going around, money is there, all you need to do is ask, but when we asked for it, the first question put to us would be 'When shall you give it back'. It was like asking a baby to run before he could even crawl and reminded me also of the chicken and egg story.

Another reason for the slow progress probably was me and my team had lost our appetite to take risks as somewhere the element of Trust had started to disappear from the organization.

Why I say trust was the reason for losing one's appetite to take risk is because when a business is run, there are some decisions which make you money and some decision which don't. When you know that your management trusts you and knows you have the best interest in your mind while taking a decision, then you feel confident.

But when the management starts looking at the good decisions you have taken with a casual attitude, like that is your job, no credit given but when the decisions goes bad, they start questioning you and your team left, right and centre, then you realize that somewhere along the path the element of Trust has disappeared. But still my team and I continued to work as much as possible with the constraints on hand.

I was fine with spending more time in Nepal and Myanmar developing these new teams, but shifting my base location out of Mumbai was something I was not willing to sacrifice, as I had stuck to this since I first started working on Nepal Project in 2008.

If given a choice to choose between Family and Work, my choice would have been crystal clear.

Initially the new management was fine with this, but probably losing patience at the slow progress, they felt the revenue generation process needed to be speeded up and hence on 3rd January 2019, I got a call from SK Sir telling me the new management wanted me to move permanently to Myanmar and were fine if I take my family with me as well and I would be adequately compensated. This they wanted me to do with immediate effect.

My thoughts went only in one direction and that was, probably the management wanted more time from me and since I could not give it, it was better I step away.

Also somewhere there was something which was missing in terms of trust, so stepping away was the best thing I could do for the new management whereby they could implement things freely the way they deemed fit and since I was been given a choice to choose between Family and Work, the choice was easy.

This conversation would have lasted barely a minute and immediately I told SK Sir in that case, I shall be sending him my resignation in the next 15 minutes with the only condition being that my last day shall be 31st March 2019. This I insisted as I needed to complete my taxation related requirements.

Like all my previous commitment, my resignation was delivered to SK Sir within 15 minutes as I carry a soft copy of my resignation always with me, very filmy right.

Another reason for me being comfortable in taking this decision was because I had achieved whatever I had set out to achieve in GL and there was nothing more I could contribute.

Since I am a strong believer of What Ever Happens, Happens for the Best" my resignation flowed easily. Like they say, Third Time is Charm and my Dilemma of moving on from GL was solved.

After putting in my resignation and even without waiting for it to get accepted, I spoke to my Country Heads in Nepal and Myanmar and informed them that I was moving on.

My official resignation acceptance came around end February but not before I met with the company MD along with CN Sir and the new management in Mumbai, where they offered to help me out if I was facing any problems and that I should look at reconsidering my decision and move to Myanmar as was being requested.

After a nice discussion, I explained why I cannot move out of India and expressed my gratitude to GL and the entire Management Team for making me what I am and for giving me so many opportunities for which I shall always be indebted.

What actually summarized my journey in GL was the farewell I received on 6th April 2019. Seeing the love and respect for me in my team's eyes, made me realize that I achieved what I had set out for and this was the perfect end to a beautiful journey which began in 2000.

Like my nature, of not looking back, I have not looked back once I left GL. I still have friends there and keep chatting with them once in a while but I have moved on as I normally do.

Moving on was easy as it fitted perfectly with my belief system and met my criteria's as well which I have listed below.

- Always Take Action Based on your priorities and since my family was my priority choice was easy

- Keep Moving On

- Do Things Which Bring You Happiness

Again this was how I managed my Work Place and was based on my belief system and my commandments. I am sure you might correlate with a few of these instances and associate them with instances in your personal life, but I am sure your actions would be based on your belief system which you have derived from your experiences.

My instances are just an illustration for helping you look at the things from your belief perspective and help you answer the two questions which made me start this journey which were,

- <u>"Why did I behave in this manner when I was faced with a particular situation?"</u> and

- <u>"Why did I choose the option I chose to come out of the situation?"</u>

I would again like you to remember the principal that 'One Size Does Not Fit All' and you need to find your own path.

The biggest reason for frustration at work places are when one is made to take decisions which actually go against what you feel is right and since one cannot always keep changing jobs, one needs to compromise somewhere to survive.

It is when the survival aspect kicks in at the cost of your belief system, frustration sets in.

The only way to handle these decisions are again simple, try and be as transparent as possible, communicating what reasons have compelled you to take the said decision and if possible handle the situation with as much empathy as you can.

To get empathy in your life there is a simple formula for that as well and that is 'One Man's Hero Is Another Man's Villain', which simply means from your point of view you might be right but from the other person who is at the receiving end of your action the feeling might be totally different.

An example for this is, if you shout on your team mate for the goof up according to you which he has done, you forgot to look at things from the perspective of your team mate who according to you has goofed up.

It could so happen that in the mind of your team mate, the reason he goofed up was because you did not train him or gave him inadequate instructions. In this instance you are the Hero from your perspective but from your team mates viewpoint you are the villain.

Not easy to think that you might be a villain in someone's life, but believe me there will be a number of instances when you will be the villain in someone's life, and that is something you cannot avoid.

The only way, you survive this is by being true to yourself and understand this concept of empathy.

If you are able to do this, then I guarantee you that you shall be successful at your work place and your frustration level shall be greatly under control.

The value of my guarantee is however limited to 10% of the value of the book which you have bought.

My disclaimer is, 'Please do not literally take my solutions and follow it blindly, but come up with your own special ones'

My Work Place Journey continues still…… but in a different context and scenario.

Chapter 12 - Managing And Nurturing Children

Family and Work Place Management I have already touched upon, but there is another aspect of the family which affects your happiness and since it affects your Happiness it has a direct correlation to all your other aspects of your life as well and therefore this also needs to be managed.

The concept of 'Hero and Villain' is again a very valid concept when it comes to parenting.

There is a famous saying in India which is "Jab Tum Baap Banoge Toh Tumhe Pata Chalega", which simply means 'When you become a Father then you will realize'.

When we were kids, we heard this all the time from our parents when we nagged them and now when our kids nag us we exactly say the same things. The chain keeps going on continuously.

Hopefully by reading this chapter you will find a way of breaking this chain as a parent and similarly even if the chain is not broken at least you shall be aware that a chain exists. Kid's reading this chapter shall also probably understand why their parents say what they say.

As per me, the most important thing when it comes to handling kids is, to understand that we as parents do have an effect on what our kids become. As I have mentioned in the very beginning of this book that a child is like a mould ready to be cast and we as parents do play an important part in what the child becomes.

There is a reason why it is said that you should not fight or curse or use foul language in front of kids as kids pick these things up easily and since their parents or elders were doing it, he/she finds this behaviour is acceptable and starts subconsciously adapting it in his/her life.

We also end up doing another thing and that is we start living our kids' lives. We tell them what to do, we tell them what not to do, we tell them what to eat, we tell them what to play, we tell them what to study, we tell them what not to study, we tell them, we tell them, we tell them......

It is as if, since we could not do it, they need to do it or since we did it, they need to do it as well. We forget one important thing in this regard that every child as is the case with our elders, or cousins or spouse is a distinct entity in their own regard and they have a mind of their own and their mind will pick up things based on their experiences in life and they shall develop their own personality and their own belief systems.

Instead of letting the child be its own person we start commanding things in its life to such an extent that the child loses himself.

We need to discipline a child and tell him/her what is good or bad but we need to tell him/her this through the experiences he/she has. We can become an example to them, but whether they want to follow that example is up to them to decide.

I strongly believe we cannot protect our kids from everything in the world, so we need to let them be free to explore the world. I respect my father and mother for this a lot. They never stopped me, yes there were issues and I was also spanked a few times by my father and almost all the time by my mother when I behaved badly, but that is part and parcel of the Indian methodology of raising a child.

My parents were never over protective about me, as can be seen in the instances when I travelled alone since the age of 15 playing matches in many parts of India like Bhusawal, Kolhapur, Lucknow, Nagpur and Jalna. They helped me overcome the fear of travelling alone by allowing me to experience it.

They never forced me to do anything, but probably they knew me better than I did myself, as I never misused their freedom.

The way I learnt swimming was similar too. Satish Jijajee's brother had come down to Mumbai and we had gone to the sports club where my father was a member, for swimming. Satish Jijajee's brother asked me a question as to whether I knew swimming and when I said, I have had a few lessons but I was not confident, he just picked me up and threw me in at the deep end.

Here I was grasping for breath but I managed to swim to the edge and get out. Once I was out, he asked me, "Ho Gaya Na", 'You Did It'. He had managed to get the fear of drowning out of me and then it was all smooth swimming from that day onwards.

This lesson also became the basis of me not getting scared in life as I knew how to swim in life which was by way of adapting.

It is all because of my upbringing which gives me the confidence to advise you in this regard.

Saying all these things you will say is easy, but implementing and letting go in today's time is difficult, which again I beg to differ is not so. I don't know what my kids shall develop into, but I do know one thing and that is I cannot live their lives.

My eldest son Shreesh is now 20 years old. He is a personality in himself with his own belief system. He has picked up a few traits from me and Meeta but has also picked up a few traits from his other elders and cousins as well.

Prithvi, who is 10 years at the time I am writing this book, is just starting to express himself and one thing which is clear to both Meeta and me is that both Shreesh and Prithvi are two different individuals, having separate traits and characteristics.

Shreesh is an Introvert, probably like me with a very small close set of friends, probably influenced by the fact, that like me we shifted him from one school to another when he was growing up.

We tried to correct this with Prithvi by keeping him in one school only, at least till now.

Shreesh on his part has started acting as Prithvi's guardian and is very protective about him, like I and Meeta are with our cousins, brothers and sisters. One more thing which shows Shreesh is more like Meeta is his inquisitiveness. He likes to acquire knowledge about everything and anything and is much more tech savvy than I shall ever be, but he cannot stick himself to do one thing. I am told I have lots of patience and can sit doing a single job continuously for a long period of time, but Meeta does not have that much patience and so I think Shreesh is more like her.

The aspect which people say he resembles both of us in, is the way he loves and respect his family. He is very comfortable with all of them. Even his cousins some of whom are at least 12-15 years elder to him, he gets along well with them. Like it is said often it is in your genes, and being happy with our families is in our genes.

No one is perfect and definitely not me, as Shreesh would know better. It is not good to hit a child, but I have lost my cool on Shreesh and he has been at the receiving end of a good spanking from me on a couple of occasions. But one thing Shreesh will agree also is that after he has got a spanking from me, he also gets an emotional speech from my side and if his mood is fine, then a hug from me as well.

Prithvi also on his part, has got up to now, one good spanking from my side, and a few good 4-5 emotional lectures, which he hears, without understanding anything that I have said.

There have been lots of challenges which Meeta and I have faced with Shreesh, a couple I shall list down for your reference as they have had a potential of exploding and how we managed it using our belief system.

CH 12.1 - How We Overcame The Challenge To Convince Shreesh to Pursue His Engineering In India, Dubai or Singapore instead of US and UK

Shreesh after passing out his 10th grade with decent marks expressed his desire to take up Engineering as his preferred graduation programme and accordingly picked up subjects in his Plus 2 program. Once he completed his plus 12th, he said he was firm on his desire to take up Engineering and expressed his desire to move to US or UK to pursue his graduation program.

The one thing which Meeta and I were clear about was, although we were fine with Shreesh doing his Engineering, we were uncomfortable in him going as far away as UK or US to do it, at least till his graduation level, post-graduation we were ok with him pursuing in US or UK. The reason we were not comfortable of sending Shreesh to US or UK was we were not convinced he was mature enough to handle both the physical distance and being independent part together.

We made him sit down and requested him to choose his college in and around India. Since Vipra was there in Singapore we were comfortable with Shreesh going there as well or Dubai which was just a couple of hours flight from Mumbai. We left the decision to Shreesh to decide but I did give him my budget which I could afford for his yearly fees and said according to this budget he can choose his college.

Shreesh chose his preferred college after visiting a couple of campuses and my support to him was there throughout. We completed his joining formalities and happily sent him off to pursue his course.

While handling this situation with Shreesh, both Meeta and I Stuck to our core belief systems and

- Respected Shreesh's decisions,

- But at the same time did not bend backwards to fulfil his every desire, thereby telling him, although he is in control of his life, he needs to be financially prudent as well.

CH 12.2 - How We Overcame The Challenge When Shreesh Expressed his Desire to Quit Engineering and become an Entrepreneur

During Shreesh's first year in college, a bug of setting up his own business bit him. He developed his idea and also presented it to me and his faculty as well. His idea was appreciated and he was inducted to the Entrepreneurs club in his college which was essentially a group of students who have come up with ideas which they would like to pursue and take forward after their graduations.

They were allowed to take help from their fellow college mates and faculty if they so needed and there were forums where they could pitch their ideas to Industry Veterans as well to seek their investments in their idea.

Once the desire of becoming an Entrepreneur came into him and combined with India's Engineering System which had not changed in decades, Shreesh lost all interest in his desire to become an Engineer.

Initially, he did not confide in me, but finally got the courage to tell me that he did not want to pursue Engineering and wanted to take up an Entrepreneurial Course in Mumbai which he had found out about.

Initially as all Father's I too tried to convince him to continue, by advising him that after his Engineering he could take up an MBA course and then set up his business and this way he shall have various options in his life open.

The scene from 3 Idiots was being repeated in our family, with me being Parikshit Sahani and Shreesh being R Madhavan.

Since we respected Shreesh's decision we allowed him to quit Engineering but requested him to complete his first year.

He completed his first year as we had requested and like I did with Shreesh when it came to picking his Engineering College, I asked Shreesh to finalize his next college and complete all his formalities for his new college as well.

You will think what sort of parents we are allowing our son to drop out in first year itself. But all we were doing was being true to ourselves.

The one thing which was made absolutely clear to Shreesh was he can become an entrepreneur but he will need to complete his graduation in any field he chooses at the same time. So it was not like a free pass was being given to him.

While handling this situation with Shreesh, both Meeta and I Stuck to our core belief systems and

- Respected Shreesh's decisions,
- Allowed his Self-Belief to develop

- But it was told to him that there is a limit up to which he shall be given his freedom

Was this the best handling of the situation only time will tell but at least, I have given Shreesh the best lesson of his life and that is I have tried to make him realize that he needs to take decisions from his perspective and live with it.

I am sure when you ask Shreesh, whether I was a good parent, he shall tell you, 50:50, and he would also say he would have liked his father to be more open with him and also a little bit more friendlier.

He does not know the reason why I cannot be friendlier or open with him but hopefully, once he reads this book he shall understand me a little better. This is one more reason for writing this book.

There is a saying which I see a lot of youngsters say, "We Are What We Are", to which my reply is "Like You Are What You Are", "I Am What I Am"

I am sure as parents or as kids just starting their careers you will identify with these sets of problems but like I have said many a times earlier as well, one size does not fit all, you need to be mindful that your actions have to be based on your belief system and not mine.

Just trying to avoid becoming Villains in your kid's life in today's world, is the solution to avoiding frustration coming across in your life when it comes to your Kids Management problem and this I guarantee.

The value of my guarantee is however limited to 10% of the value of the book which you have bought.

My disclaimer is, 'Please do not literally take my solutions and follow it blindly, but come up with your own special solutions of how you can avoid the Hero – Villain dilemma'

Chapter 13 - Adjusting to Our Society

We all are social animals, and we need our society to survive and therefore how one adjusts to his society is equally important. Adjusting to the society one lives in provides the stability one needs to survive and be happy.

But first things first, how did I become aware of the fact that one needs to adapt and adjust to the society he/she lives in to be happy?

I realized this when I started getting affected by the news from India and how the commentary was happening in India post 2011. Since it was impacting me, I decided to dig deeper to find the reason behind it.

The "India against Corruption" movement was happening, the various scandals like Telecom 2G, Commonwealth Games, followed by scandal after scandal were exposed in front of us every day by the 24 x 7 news channels who kept on giving the same news, over and over again.

Till this point of time, my world was limited to My Family, My Friends and My Work. But since the social media was discovered by the politicians in 2012, the period of 2012 to 2014 was as if a war had broken out, not in the real world but the social media world, with accusations flying left right and centre and entering my life in a big way.

The 2014 elections whose preparation started from 2011, felt as if it was the deciding elections of all elections which was taking place in India and it was as if every Indian was being pulled into this war with the bombardment of social messages on all platforms.

Whether you open a You Tube App or a Facebook App, it was as if the only thing which was happening was the Indian Elections and the only messages being conveyed were either Modi Ji's Message of 'Aache Din Ayenge', 'Good Days Will Come' or the bombardment of Corruption scandals against the UPA Government.

Families were being split down in the middle depending on which side of the debate you were on and since families started getting divided, the society too was getting divided and this reminded me of my Saudi days.

Since these debates which happen in the society affects you and you cannot live without your society, the concept of Society Management came into my head.

Now that I realized that I needed to manage and adjust to the society I lived in, I needed to get some more information. Information on What was happening in my society and why?

The period of 2012 to 2014 was just crazy and it continues to be crazy even today and the Great War although won is still going on every day in the Media and the Digital world.

Owing to my belief system I started listening to the debates, not the ones on TV, but the ones which were happening on the social media, amongst the intellectuals who were renowned from both sides of the divide.

I was also attracted towards understanding religion and what all it denoted during this period. This attraction was because more often than not, the fight between those who supported Modi Ji and those who don't support him, was on religious lines

Being a Hindu, I said to myself let me first learn what Hinduism means not only from a spiritual perspective but from a historical perspective as well.

While scouting through the internet, I came across a 4 hour lecture given by Professor Sandeep Manudhane to his students who were appearing for their IAS exams. The explanation given by him effectively summarized the Sanatan Philosophy. There are other beautiful lectures on world history and Religion from the same set of professors including Sandeep Ji, but they are purely fact based and hence they are useful to people who seek pure knowledge.

Another reason for relying on these lectures was because these lectures were given to our future IAS/IPS/IFS/IRS Officers who had to study these topics as they were a part of their exams.

After hearing this lecture you can check out what others have also said. Similarly my strong recommendation is before judging other religions, you need to study them in details and also understand the faith and logic behind their origin. This is just my advice, don't take it seriously.

Through these debates and a little online research I realized something profound. Nothing actually changes in a society. The society we live in has not changed for centuries. Superficially, things feel modern, but inside the core of the society everything remains the same.

The Indian elections helped to prove this. I thought once the elections were over, the dream world promised would be achieved. After years of boxed up coalitions struggling for power, we finally had a single party government with a strong leader and probably now finally we shall see the change promised after Independence.

However, there has been absolutely no difference in what my life was before and after 2014 elections. The Great War although won by Modi ji, had no impact on my life. Everything remained the same, the only difference being from having a prime minister who rarely spoke, we got a prime minister who always speaks 'His Maan Ki Baat'.

Media, I am told is a reflection of the society as it exists. It provides a mirror to the society and shows the various facets of the society. From good to bad, from beautiful to ugly, this is what I had thought. But something strange started to happen with the media prior and post 2014. They were the only other thing which changed actually.

Prior to 2014, media was always questioning those in power, but after 2014, media was questioning the people who were thrown out of power for their corruption and continue to do even after 6 years of they being out of power at the time of me writing this. It was as if India had changed from a corrupt country where living a life was difficult, to a country where life was a bed of roses, no corruption, jobs all around, everyone happy and everyone working for the betterment of the country, it was like a dreamland as the people in power and in the media made us believe.

I was in a unique position as I used to spend close to 20 days outside India and 10 days within India and I was seeing both sides of the coin. Because of me being able to see both sides of the coin, I could not get myself to digest how as per the world, as per the media, as per the NRI's , India had changed, while as per me, my life in India remained unchanged during the 10 days I lived here.

Yes there was Demonetization and Yes there was GST but Demonetization was already done in the past and even as recently in 2014, when 500 Rupees notes issued prior to 2005 were demonetized and GST was in the pipeline since 2003 and every central government wanted it while all state governments did not as the states would have been the biggest losers in the implementation of GST.

I still needed to go across to the same set of officers in the machinery to get my license to do business, the only change being from physically going there I had to go online, so cost increased as Internet Bandwidth added to my overheads, besides this I still had to entertain the officer of the concerned department.

To pay the taxes whether GST / Income tax, I still needed to go across to the Tax guys and file my returns through my CA as laws became more complicated with more compliances being thrown in, as we are all corrupt and the system needs these compliances to ensure that corruption is reduced. So my cost increased on two fronts, CA + Accountant + Internet Bandwidth.

Yes there was no news of corruption but similarly all the corruption cases, which were the talk of the town, previously disappeared. No convictions whatsoever as if there was no corruption at all. I still needed to handle the local traffic cop and his requirements as his salary remains too less and he still has nowhere else to go but come to us for his support.

I could not understand why the Media which is the mirror of the society did not see that life had not changed. The only explanation I have for this attitude of the media could be 'Look at the Bright Side Dear, Look at the Bright Side'. Now at least on paper India is a better country to live in.

Now as that gave me some answers which I was looking for, let's go about answering the question of how one can manage a society.

The easy answer is all we need to do to manage the society we live in is, accept all the norms the society lays down and follow it without questioning it.

The difficult answer of how one can manage a society is a painful and long one, and I am sure you will not be interested in it, but me being me, I shall try and give you the long answer as well with a safe harbour again "PLEASE DO NOT TAKE IT SERIOUSLY", choice however remains yours which you shall choose.

Since society is made up of people just like us and it is like a collective conscious, all one needs to do is understand essentially what a society is made up of and What its components are? And hence adapt accordingly to it.

Sounds simple, Yes, but believe me it is very difficult.

But if you want to follow the difficult path of understanding society as to what it is and then adjust to it, boy you are in for a lot of surprises. Even great scholars have failed to understand this great mystery, so how can a simple man like me try and answer this question.

But me being me, I Need To Say What I Have To Say, So Here Goes The Long, Tough, Often Difficult, Out Rightly Ludicrous Answer To The Question Of Understanding Society. I would again like to take a Safe Harbour here *"PLEASE DISREGARD WHAT EVER YOU READ FROM HERE ONWARDS TO THE END OF THIS CHAPTER"*

As per me the society is made up of 3 categories of people,

- The Rulers

- The Ruled

- The Irrelevant

The Rulers in a society in olden times were the kings and queens which are now replaced by the Quarter of Politicians, Bureaucrats, Law Implementing Machinery and Big Business Houses who have become so big that their collapse shall pull the trio of Politicians, Bureaucrats and Law Implementing Machinery down with them.

The Ruled are the people who follow laws because they are too scared to break them as they have everything or something to lose if they are hauled up. They are the Small Businessman, Middle Class – Both Upper and Lower, Farmers who own some land or have some assets like a house, Labourers who again own some asset like a house etc.

The Irrelevant are those who own nothing, they survive on a day to day basis and in general have nothing to lose.

The mix of the people in any average society is

- 1%-2% is in the Rulers Category,

- 60%-70% are those in the Ruled Category

- And around 28% - 40% in the Irrelevant Category.

Now since I have laid down the basics on what a society normally comprises of let me look at each set of people from a perspective of space they occupy and why I consider them in the category, as I do.

In the modern world, The Rulers are those people you devise laws and implement them in a democracy and their actions affect millions and millions of people and hence they are the Rulers.

The Ruled are the ruled because laws are primarily made to keep these set of people under control as they are the biggest threats to the Rulers and they need to be kept in check to ensure they don't rebel.

Those who have nothing, what Rules will you apply to them hence they are the Irrelevant Group.

Between the Ruled and The Irrelevant, The Irrelevant are the easiest to manage for a Politician and Bureaucrats as they become Happy with small things they receive as they are used to getting nothing from the society they live in.

I sincerely hope there is no conflict on this logic of classification as otherwise; whatever I am going to write after this will be totally irrelevant.

Once you understand and accept this logic the next question which needs to be answered is can there be an interchange in roles between the Rulers, the Ruled and the Irrelevant People.

The ideal answer should be yes, but this is not an ideal world and the answer to the question of upward mobility or downward mobility is very rare. Once in a blue moon it happens that a nobody can become a somebody, rare but it does happen at times and that is why we celebrate it, in a big way. But most of the time the status quo is maintained.

So why does the status quo between the Rulers, Ruled and Irrelevant remain. Another Million Dollar Question Right?.

I found the starting point of my answer in a very unlikely place.

It was while browsing through the Internet; I came across a programme in which Devdutt Pattanaik ji was being interviewed for a business channel. In this programme Pattanaik ji was classifying people on the lines of Lord Krishna, Lord Ram, Ravana and Dhuryodhan to put his point across.

Lord Krishna was high on principals but was ready to break rules if it meant protecting his principals.

Lord Ram was high on principals and high on rules as well, that is why always sacrificing for his loved ones.

Then there are the people who are low on principals and

also low on rules basically the Ravana type as depicted by Ramanand Sagar ji

And finally there are the people who were like low on principals but high on rules, people for whom rules matter while principals can be discarded, people like Dhuryodhan as depicted by B R Chopra ji.

Devdutt ji was using this example to classify employees in an organization to show why only a few succeed in business and life and why a majority fail.

I tried to use the Analogy of Devdutt ji, and came up with my analogy of why the status quo remains as it does.

I twisted this logic of Devdutt ji slightly by putting people such as Steve Jobs, Bill Gates, Dhirubhai Ambani in the category of rebels who broke rules like you need to have a degree, you need to be rich to succeed and still succeeded because they stuck to their principals of doing things differently and at the end of the day creating value.

Similarly, I placed the bureaucrats, politicians and judiciary of the world in the category of people who are always sticking to rules forgetting the most important principal as to why they are in these roles and that is to serve and protect the people.

I am in no way criticizing the bureaucrats, politicians and judiciary of the world, all I am saying they needed to be the Lord Rams of the world but because they have forgotten the main principal i.e. they need to work for the people, they have become the Dhuryodhan's of the world at present.

So when I started thinking a little more on this I also realized, I had found my answers as to why nothing changed in spite the Great War Being Over and why the Media of today had stopped questioning those in power.

As per my analysis, which I state very clearly "PLEASE DO NOT TAKE SERIOUSLY', the Status Quo is maintained because of 3 reasons which I have tried to list down below,

- The Principle Of Karma which should keep us on the right side of the law but does not

- My Hypothesis on we 'Being Homogenous'

- 'We Indians are a Breed Apart' which should contradict the Homogenous Hypothesis but strangely does not

CH 13.1 - KARMA - The Principle which should keep us on the right side of the law but does not

We Indians believe in the principal of Karma Big Way. For us everything which connects us to our Vedic Past is very important and The Logic is Karma is one of the oldest we have.

My understanding of Karma and its beginnings, is however slightly different from what is normally understood in the Indian context.

'As the human civilization grew, people with evolved thinking looked at answers to;

- How as part of a community one should live their lives?

- How should one behave with others?

- What should be the rules under which a community of people should start living? Etc. ….

Over a period of thousands of years one such thought process which evolved was the concept of Rightful Living.

The common thread that connected every religion in the world whether it is Hinduism, Judaism, Zoroastrianism, Jainism, Christianity, Islam, Sikhism which are today in practice was the concept of doing the right thing and living a Righteous Life.

Our scholars, some of them with far greater insights and truly enlightened in the knowledge of their experiences, understood human psychology very well and put across these principles of rightful living for all of us to follow.

This path of rightful living needed to have an outcome and the outcome was defined as enlightenment in some religions and was defined as heaven in some other religions.

Since there was a reward at the end of the journey which was rightfully lived, there needed to be repercussions for a life lived away from this rightful path and hence came the concept of judgement. The more good things than bad things you did in your life, the better your chances of getting a favourable result on judgement day.

By installing a fear of judgement day our scholars wanted to put us on the righteous path and therefore gave us this wonderful principle of KARMA – Do good and good shall come to you,

Do bad and bad shall come to you, but what they actually wanted to tell us was '*__Always Do The Right Thing__*'.

The logic of KARMA provides one with a way of internalizing the issues at hand and tries to enable one to cope with the issues by making one focus on their own actions rather than externalizing the issue and making other people responsible for the things happening to you, thereby preventing social unrest and discomfort in the community.

Our scholars knew that this was the best way to keep our animal instincts under control and therefore gave us this wonderful Logic of KARMA.

Our scholars also understood that each person was different so they broke down the population into categories like Teachers, Warriors, Traders and Workers and accordingly started providing work to them to ensure that there was progress in the civilization. J.K. Rowling also used this logic in her Harry Potter Series to classify the kids when they joined the magic school.

There was supposed to be no restriction between movements within the categories, any person based on he/she having the skills for the required category could move from one category to other.

The scholars however relied on the goodness of the leaders, kings, teachers to implement the correct principle of KARMA and ensure there is no deprivation of opportunities to people.

Unfortunately, when the people responsible for implementing this beautiful principle become corrupt, this Logic of Karma – becomes a curse. The path of Righteousness is forgotten and it is substituted by Oppression.

A Ruler whose children did not exhibit the quality of a ruler but that of a worker, a warrior whose children did not exhibit the quality of a warrior but that of a teacher, probably found it difficult to digest that his children were different from him/her, so instead of stepping down as rulers or warriors and giving someone else who is more capable the right to rule or become a warrior, they changed the entire logic to justify the protection of their loved ones.

Being born in a house of a ruler meant you have done something good in your previous life and therefore had the right to live the life of privileges and a person born into a poor family was born poor because of his/her past actions too and hence he needs to suffer in this life.

If you are already judged and you are again given the human form and human form being the most pure, then what is this logic of the past effecting your future, contradictory right?

This Right By Birth Concept, was nothing but a way of protecting the space created by people who are in the upper layer and ensure that layer or space was passed on to their kin, because our inherent nature is to protect our loved ones.

This ensured that when you see a poor person, instead of trying to help them, you just move ahead in life by telling yourself this is his KARMA. When you see a person diseased you say to yourself that the person is suffering because of his / her own past deeds and move on.

Our scholars and all our Religious Texts tried to tell us not to harm fellow beings, be one with nature, focus on intellect and not colour / caste / creed and not be materialistic. They created fables, stories to inculcate morals in us and tried to create a system that propagated being good.

Over generations, like everything gets corrupted, we Indians also got corrupted as did the rest of the world.

Instead of following the Righteous Path advocated by our scholars, we started following the Birth Concept of Karma; all this to protect the spaces in power created by the privileged over generations and that is why KARMA – The principle which should have kept us on the right side of the law was used to justify all the wrongs.

Giving you an example,

- We bribe people, but justify it in our mind as a system of barter. He gives us something in return and therefore we need to give him something. Not realising that probably since we are rich and can bribe our way out, we are not allowing space to some other more deserving person who cannot bribe. All we are doing by Bribing is ensuring our space gets protected.

- People take Bribes, justify it to themselves with the logic so what, everyone takes bribes and we are taking from people who anyway have extra to give so what is the harm. Not realizing that taking this bribe is ensuring that the rich remain rich and the poor who cannot remain poor.

How many generations of Politicians you see in Politics, similarly how many generations of IAS / IPS / IFS / IRS / Lawyers / Judges do you see, how many generation of Bureaucrats do you see.

The lecture on Hinduism which I referred above is supposed to be heard by every Indian Bureaucrat whether IAS/IPS etc., but do they advise the Politicians when they say things contrary to what actual Hinduism is, they don't.

One after the other, one generation after the other, all rising to the top and in some way or the other ensuring the space created is protected. Similarly see Business Houses, all the same always the same. This is not only in India, it is across the globe.

Since Media was the only source which can show their True Faces, the first thing which any ruler does is, they try and suffocate it. Free Speech is a dream and like all dreams, it is not a reality.

This is one part of the Answer of how the status quo is maintained using the Concept of Karma to protect the space which a Ruler occupied from the Ruled and the Irrelevant.

But then you will ask why the Ruled and Irrelevant do not rise against the Rulers. To this comes the next part.

CH 13.2 - Hypothesis on 'Being Homogenous'

I first touched base on this hypothesis in Chapter 11, and I have again produced it below,

- 'We Humans love living in a homogenous environment, if however we come across someone or something which threatens to break this homogeneity, we fight it back. Initially, we fight through discussion to convince him or her to again rethink their positions and if still he or she continues on the path of thinking differently, we then threaten to throw them out of our group and even if this does not work then the majority destroys them entirely to protect their homogeneity'

Since we love being Homogenous, we resent if someone or something changes.

If we see someone standing at the red light in the middle of the night, we think what an idiot he/she is following the rule and ensure we honk at him/her and ensure they break the signal or give them a piece of their mind for making them wait as well.

Similarly when we see some businessman who is trying to follow all rules and comply with all requirements, we push such businessman up the wall with a barrage of compliances which have been devised in a manner to ensure somewhere or the other he/she shall falter and then the local politician, or bureaucrat or local officer can step in and make a quick buck.

Similarly if we see someone from a poor background coming up we praise his efforts, but we do not invite him to our house or get him married in to our family.

Similarly if we see someone questioning the laid down practices of discrimination, we ensure either he/she is convinced to change their thinking or are managed in a way so they stop raising their voices.

There are rules governing discrimination in India, but does the Politician, Bureaucrats or Law Enforcing Machinery implement them the way they implement the law when it comes to someone breaking the signal or someone doing some tax evasion and actually goes all out in protecting the people raising their voices against discrimination.

The answer to why Politicians, Bureaucrats or Law Enforcing Machinery does not protect these voices in the same manner is the answer to the question How the Status Quo Is Maintained and Why No Change after 2014 also.

Ask any Politicians to become one with us and give up his perks especially the ones they enjoy after their term ends and you will see all Politicians ganging up together objecting to it.

Ask a Bureaucrat to work for the people and for his salary he gets and not take any perks post retirement as general public do and you will see all Bureaucrats across the State, Centre, Categories, come together to object to it.

Ask a person in the Police or Judiciary to provide time bound justice and you will find out that they shall have 10 reasons why they cannot and all that in the name of justice.

A person who has done something wrong knows what he has done and the only way he can survive now is by delaying getting caught and if caught, delaying justice being served. Everyone knows this but do they do anything about it and here lies your answer.

Ask a Businessman to follow all rules and not pay anything to the Politician, Bureaucrats and instead spend this amount for the welfare of his staff and 'YOU SHALL GET YOUR ANSWER AS TO WHY THINGS DO NOT CHANGE'.

The Rulers are a Homogenous Unit and they shall not tolerate anyone trying to break their homogeneity and hence No Change. They also have the entire system behind them and since the Ruled have something to lose; they also prefer the same set of Rulers to continue as otherwise they shall get in to trouble if they challenge them. The Irrelevant are anyways the most easiest to manage as giving them free perks ensures that they don't think and are happy that at least someone thought about them.

Both the Ruled and the Irrelevant realize that they are being used but the homogeneity principal applies to them as well as it does to the Rulers.

When a small businessman starts following the rules and becomes successful, it is invariably his competitor only who complains against this honest businessman to the Rulers and ensures he is bombarded by the Rulers to become like one of the other corrupt businessmen in society.

Similarly when a poor person because of his efforts tries to rise up in society, the first battle which such a person has to face is his own community which he belongs to and then if he is successful in defeating his own people, he goes on to fight the Rulers and by this time, most of them just give up.

Now comes the part when I touch base on the third reason how the Status Quo is maintained.

CH 13.3 - Why 'Indians Are A Breed Apart'

Now you will say since we are a Homogenous Unit and we don't allow rebels to rise up within our ranks how come my hypothesis of we 'Indians are a Breed Apart' is valid. Well both are the same once you have read on.

To better explain this concept to you, I am replacing the Ruler to an Employee and I am changing the Democratic Society we live in to an Organization were the Employee works. Since the Ruler is afraid he can be replaced in a Democratic Set Up, an employee is also always afraid that he can be replaced.

To make you understand what I am driving towards, first of all I shall take you to my experiences which I had in India and Saudi while executing the NL, RL Projects in India and the

STC Project in Saudi, the job was the same but there were two sets of management styles in play.

In STC and NL projects the management team comprised of Europeans while in RL our dealings were with pure Indians, born and brought up in India. Before you go further I would like to make a Safe Harbour 'PLEASE DON'T CONSIDER THIS HYPOTHESIS SERIOUSLY'

The concept of the Europeans was simple, everyone needs to survive and for everyone to survive everyone needs to make money, therefore they never insisted on low prices. They believed if you are doing business then you need to make decent margin so that you don't compromise with quality.

However, when it came to Indian People in Management of RL or somewhere else, the logic changed. It was always why do you need to make money, we are giving you enough for you to survive so be happy. This made me realize one thing about us Indians. We are very cut throat people; we will do anything to succeed in our job. Look at the world almost everywhere you will find Indians at top positions. This is because we are ruthless when it comes to our jobs. Since we are 130 crores, we have had to struggle all our lives, right from the day we are born to the day we die, we need to fight to survive, so we know how to survive.

Why I say since we are born is because we have a 3% mortality rate when the world over it is only 0.3%, so just surviving our first few months is difficult.

If we somehow survive this we still have to face malnutrition with over 30% of Indian children having nutritional deficiencies.

Even if we survive this and reach school, we have to fight for getting admission in a decent school in spite of Right to Education mandated in our constitution.

If we somehow get admission still only 30% of the children entering the education stream pass graduation level.

If somehow we graduate, then only around 60% of those who graduate get decent jobs.

So you understand why, when we get a decent job, we fight really hard to stay in it, unless it is a Government Job. Since we are also lazy at the same time we love to get into a Government Job.

In India we are brought up to compete. Our education system rewards the cut throat culture and to succeed you have to beat everyone else.

Now when I say till we die, is because death in India is also not easy as Elders, are left on their own as their children cannot take care of them, Governments have no money to spare to take care of them, insurance company do not give senior citizens medical cover after they cross 65.

So if you grow old in India, only way you shall die peacefully is if your family has been influenced by the teachings of Ramanand Sagar ji and B R Chopra ji.

Although, I am an Indian, when I see an Indian across the negotiating table I know what to expect and I have to be always on my guard as I am sure he has an ace up his sleeve somewhere which he shall use to benefit his company at my cost so that he can earn brownie points with his management and stay safe in his job.

He too knows I too have an ace up my sleeve somewhere as well as he knows I am an Indian as well and therefore the one thing which gets missed out is this is the element of Trust. With an Indian across the table, it is always a transactional deal, never a relationship builder.

My Saudi experience of executing project and my India experience of executing projects were also totally different. We were executing the same Turn Key job both places, but the experiences were totally contradictory. Indians were executing the project in Saudi and it was an Indian who was executing in India, but their behaviour was totally different.

This led to my next part of my hypothesis which is listed below and that too you should 'DISREGARD'.

In Saudi, processes were followed and instructions implemented without questioning them, while in India the same set of instructions were disregarded and any push for implementing processes was totally side lined. Giving you an example which is as simple as keep all documents related to a site in a single folder for easy access and review. This was implemented beautifully in Saudi Arabia but when it came to implementing the same thing in India, except for the final set of documents mandated for claiming the final 10% of the site value, the site folder was invariable empty of any other information.

Another example but this time from how even our customers are different. In Saudi we never needed to follow up, if the documents are submitted and invoice accepted and if the credit terms is 30 days, our payment used to come on the 30th day. But come to India on the due date the customer will never pay the full amount due. He shall negotiate on this as well.

Say your outstanding is 100, the customer shall start negotiating again with you by offering you any amount less than 100 like around 50 and only if you agree to any value lower than the 100 will he pay you any amount. This made me think again as to why we behave in this particular manner and there were some thoughts which came to my mind.

I understand the insecurity element in both the examples I have listed above. If the Site Folder is implemented 100% in India, the project resource that has completed the site would become irrelevant as all data for that site is in the folder.

The renegotiating part also I can understand as the accountant at the customers end also has to pull an ace out of his sleeve to show his management how much money he has been able to conserve and gained interest and try and get his brownie points.

But I went deeper into this as I thought there needs to be a more profound answer. So I developed the next part of my Hypothesis, which again "DO NOT TAKE SERIOUSLY"

We Indians are unique, give us a straight path and we shall never follow it. Give us a red light and we shall break it. Give us a place where we should not spit and we shall spit. Give us an instruction and we shall not follow it. But all this we shall do in India. But when we go abroad, we follow all the rules and instructions even without questioning it. The question we need to ask is why this happens with us?

From my analysis I have come up with a simple answer. Since we had a civilization which is supposed to be one of the oldest, there have been rules governing us since time immemorial.

When the rules laid down suffocated us, we rebelled and there was a change in guard. A new ruler came on board and then he laid down new set of rules. When these new rules also suffocated us, we rebelled again.

This process continued on for centuries. When the Turks and Mughals came also, it was similar. They came with their set of rules and someone or the other rebelled against them and there were wars fought to break their rule. Then came the British, with their rules and regulations and we fought them as well.

But now with the British gone, we got into something new.

We got into democracy but with the rules and systems of the British. We made our constitution which provided us with our rights but we used the British System which was designed for suppression to implement it along with the whole plethora of laws from the British Generation. This was effectively used by our Modern Rulers to keep control over the society, as they replaced the British.

We had freedom to vote and that was the only way we could keep protesting our discontent and that we faithfully continue to do by throwing out governments, the only tool in the hands of the Ruled and Irrelevant.

But because the laws which were designed to control by the British remained in spite of the many government changes, the Ruled and the Irrelevant were left with no choice but to rebel against these rules.

They showed their displeasure by not following the red light rule, spitting where they were not supposed to, litter where they were not supposed to litter, tell us not to bribe and we shall bribe, tell us not to take bribe and we shall take bribe, tell us to pay our taxes and we shall find ways in which we shall not, practice discrimination on caste, sex, religion lines when it is clearly debarred in the Constitution.

It is basic genetics. We are just genetically programed to rebel. This logic of being genetically programed is also applicable to every other human being as well as across the world, when the Rules become overbearing.

There is a word in English which we use to justify our behaviour of breaking the rules and that is "But". But he did it before, but it was always happening, but it cannot be changed as it was a practice.

Our law makers also justify the suppression system with the same "But" as things need to be kept under control. Freedom of Speech is there But you can't say this and this and this and this, you can do everything but you can't do this, this, this and this.

So you will ask why we don't rebel outside India as we are genetically programmed to rebel. This is because we are very smart as well. We are smart people and because we are smart we know that when we are abroad it is not that easy to get away with breaking the law.

Since we are very smart we also know the value of our high paying foreign jobs and we also know that there are millions of Indians waiting in the shadows to pounce on our jobs, so we become sticklers for the processes laid down as we do not want to give any other person any other opportunity to take our place. For Indians Insecurity make thy perfect.

In India we continue to rebel as we know that the person implementing the law is also an Indian. He is also genetically programmed to Rebel.

That is why we 'Indians are a Breed Apart'

The above hypothesis comes with a huge disclaimer, which is "AGAIN PLEASE DO NOT TAKE IT SERIOUSLY".

Since the Employee is scared that he will lose his job, and tries everything to protect his job, so does a Ruler. He uses every trick in the book to ensure that it is difficult for someone to replace him. That is why you will see Politicians way past the normal retirement age still clinging onto power in the guise of experience, Bureaucrats even after retirement eyeing plump post retirement placements or ensuring someone in their family joins the system along with the Law Enforcing Machinery People.

It is this insecurity of our Rulers, combined with the unique ability to rebel against the Righteous Principles laid down by our scholars and our being homogenous desires; the Status Quo is maintained all the time.

The Ruled and the Irrelevant use this concept of being a rebel, being homogenous and the principle of KARMA as well but they do so in a manner which does not change the status quo.

The Ruled and the Irrelevant break rules which are not important like tax laws, traffic laws etc. They also help the Rulers by ensuring that the laws which promote non-discrimination, religious tolerance and giving respect to other citizens are not followed.

And this, my friend is the reason why there has been no change in a common man's life after 2014 or since we got independence.

Since Media is part of the Ruled System, they have also decided that it is best to stick to the people Ruling them as they have gone through the pain of changing one set of rulers and they don't want to go through this pain again.

But since we Indians believe that life shall always get better, we keep hoping the new set of Rulers will be different, thinking that at least once in a blue moon we shall get a Ruler who shall actually work for us, not realising that unless we, the Ruled and the Irrelevant, make our Rulers work for us, nothing shall change.

<u>The Dynamics between the Rulers, the Ruled and the Irrelevant is what the society we live in is all about and once you understand this dynamics you have understood what Our</u>

<u>Society Is, and once you understand your society adjusting to it is easy, Right?</u>

Since it is easy, please do understand it and accordingly adapt to it. This way you shall ensure that you do not get frustrated with the society you live in.

Ask the NRI's to come back to India as it has become a dream world to live in and you will know that they have also understood the Indian society as I have explained above and they have also understood the society they prefer living in as they are NRI's.

Anyway, I am one of the Rule Followers, as confirmed by Sunny Boy as well, so I shall stick to the easy path of handling the society challenges and that is accepting the society as it is as I have a lot to lose and since I prefer to live in India I better be on my best behaviour, especially when it comes to the Rulers.

Like it is said in Hindi "Samundar Main Rahke, Magarmach Se Bair Nahin Karte", which when translated in English means "If you live in a sea, you don't take pot shots against the crocodile in the sea" and since I am smart, I prefer to be the Ruled, not challenging the Rulers.

But I once again make my disclaimer here and that is "DON'T TAKE WHAT I HAVE STATED ABOVE SERIOUSLY"

There is no refund if you do not agree to this chapter as this chapter was a bonus one.

Chapter 14 - Conclusion But At The Same Time A New Beginning

Now that you have gone through my journey till 2019 and also got to know me, hopefully you would have seen some resemblance of your own life in my journey.

I am sure some incidences would have reminded you of the times spent with your family, your cousins, your friends, the time you got married, had your first child, started your first job, the challenges in life and the way you overcame them. I am sure you would have seen some connection.

Even if you could not relate to my life, I am sure you would have loved to get into my life and read about it..

Like I have said at the very beginning, even if you could not relate to my stories but if I could get a laugh or a smile on your face because of my stories or if my hypothesis which I again repeat "PLEASE DO NOT TAKE IT SERIOUSLY", made you think, then I would have achieved the purpose with which I set out writing my memoirs.

During my entire story, you must have seen I have used the words luckily a lot. But believe me luck has nothing to do with where you reach in life. It is your belief system which makes you who you are, takes decisions for you and leads you forward in life.

Destiny is nothing but a result of all your actions, so when you hear statements like I got lucky, it is actually the results of the action which were taken by your belief system.

To win a lottery ticket also is a combination of your beliefs. It comprises of a person first convincing himself that he can win, then he decides to sacrifice a portion of his income to buy the ticket, then he selects which ticket he will buy. All these were actions born out of his belief system, winning the lottery is just the end result.

My reference to Ramanand Sagar ji, B R Chopra Ji, Manmohan Desai ji, Hrishikesh Mukherjee Ji and Manohar Shyam Joshi Ji in my entire journey is because, I am not a great reader, in fact after college and apart from a few workshops which I have attended, I have not read a single book in my life.

My knowledge of what is right and what is wrong, what is good and what is bad has come from the TV and Movies I have watched or the stories I have heard from my Grandmother, Mother and my other Family Members. I know they are not great sources of learnings, but for me they were the best as they taught me something and also entertained me and made me laugh.

Life is a continuous process and does not stop as we all know, so one needs to keep moving forward in life. And to do so the two most important criteria to follow is to adapt and learn and that is what I did.

You need to adapt to your environment, family, colleagues, society, situations that arise, but to adapt you need to learn about your family, colleagues, society and the situation that you are in.

Since you keep getting new and different experiences as you move ahead in life, so also your core keeps getting updated. It is like an Apple I.O.S Software, every month based on what problems are faced by Apple Phone Users, Apple sends across bug fixes to protect your phone.

Your life based on your experiences, keeps learning every time something new comes up. Your core / your belief system keep's getting updated and all you need to do is accept these changes, like you agree to the terms and conditions and then press update on your I Phone; all you need to do is accept.

So my final simple formula is,

<u>LIFE = ACCEPTANCE</u>

Accept life with all its complications and all its beauty

Now you will say again, there's nothing new in what I am saying as you already know all these formulas, to which my answer remains "IF YOU ALREADY KNOW IT THEN IMPLEMENT IT AND MAKE YOUR LIFE SIMPLE"

There is no refund available for people who already know all the answers and they need to consider this as a revision then.

<u>Till we meet again. Keep Living.</u>

<u>Keep Moving Ahead, As Change Is The Only Constant</u>

<u>And Above All Keep Discovering 'WHO YOU ARE'</u>

-   Anup G